THE SECRET TO HAPPY

UNDERSTANDING YOUR CHILD'S BEHAVIOR:
A Parent's Guide to Helping a Unique Child Thrive

Kristin Martinsen Robison, MOT, OTR/L

THE SECRET TO HAPPY
UNDERSTANDING YOUR CHILD'S BEHAVIOR: A PARENT'S
GUIDE TO HELPING A UNIQUE CHILD THRIVE

iUniverse books may be ordered through booksellers or by contacting:

iUniverse
1663 Liberty Drive
Bloomington, IN 47403
www.iuniverse.com
844-349-9409

Illustrations by Bekah Rosas
Editing by Betty Christianson Martinsen & Dr. Deborah Oliver
Cover Design by Trish Sagare

ISBN: 978-1-6632-1581-9 (sc)
ISBN: 978-1-6632-1580-2 (e)

Library of Congress Control Number: 2020925809

Print information available on the last page.

iUniverse rev. date 02/17/2021

For Jens and Annika…. who made me the mom I am and taught me to be the therapist I am today. To Drew, who went along with my parenting style even though it wasn't written in a best seller and who supported me with all my ideas every step of the way. And finally, to *my* mom who taught me kindness trumps all… she is amazing, strong and the queen of "survival."

When we can all begin to consider the why behind behavior, maybe we can react differently… not with excuses or anger, but an open mind and heart. This is how I strive to live my life and what I hope to teach my children because this truly is
The Secret to Happy

THE SECRET TO HAPPY: AN INTRODUCTION

I believe that the secret to Happy is about understanding. Of course, the way we engage with one another is critical, but it all starts with how we perceive someone's behavior. When we can look at anyone and think *WHY,* it allows us to slow down, consider the human behind the behavior and maybe this will increase our compassion. So, I believe that the secret to Happy is found in each other, but this has to involve the ability to consider different explanations for why people behave the way they do.

Let me start by saying, this book is not like other books you have read. Parenting and managing behavior cannot be approached in a linear fashion and this book is about parenting and behavior. These pages are full of ideas and different considerations that will impact your perspective of what you are seeing in your child. This will directly affect how you respond to your child. The flow of this book is different; there are detours and explanations of possibility because of the myriad of interrelated concepts. We can't expect to pull out a magic book, perform step one, then two and then presto, all is fixed. Unfortunately, parenting just doesn't work like that.

The content in these pages is meant to be a companion, delivered in a way that is hopefully comical too, because honestly once you've started the miraculous, yet challenging road of parenthood, you have to make light of some things or you will make yourself crazy.

I have wished for *the* parenting crystal ball for years. Something that could tell me *why* my child is doing something, and then just as essential, *what* I can do about it. If you have more than one child, you already know that what works for one likely doesn't work for the other. There are hundreds of incredible resources out there that serve as handbooks, but one divine, all-knowing source or crystal ball would sure be fun!

Behavior is a critical communication tool. We can often figure out what is going on by reading behavior; it can help us understand the *why* of a situation and maybe even how to help. Happy matters. To find the source of Happy, The Secret to Happy, we have to know about the puzzle pieces that impact behavior every day.

THIS IS A JOURNEY

It is time to figure out the puzzle and put on a different shade of lens if we are going to change our perspective of behavior. As an occupational therapist, I have always been fascinated with the *why* of behavior. Children are especially interesting because they haven't learned to fake it, so sometimes just their behavior alone can tell us *exactly* what is going on. They show raw emotion, stumble without social refinement, and can't help but *show* us and everyone around them how they are feeling inside.

You need to remember in every challenging moment that *your child is amazing*. There is purpose to every person. Sometimes our child may look very different than we thought they should. They may be very different than you are, or your other child, or their peers. When your see your child struggle, it is easy to feel completely alone... but I promise you are not alone on this journey. We need each other now, more than ever.

This book will introduce you to some of the possible *whys* that make life hard for kids today. Some are related to their wiring and who our kiddo came into this world to be. Some can be related to how they process sensory information, or signals, which can completely elude us and prevent us from seeing the whole picture. The one *why* that applies to *all* children is related to skills which means we have to look at brain development. All of this will be discussed. There are strategies, tools, and various approaches I have found that really help.

It might be time to adjust our glasses a bit.

Thank you for taking this journey. I hope this book enlightens and encourages you.

CONTENTS

FOREWORD

Perception is the beginning and it is affected by many concepts or pieces of the puzzle. Perception is how you look at the world, behavior, yourself, and your child. Some of the things that affect your perception include previous failures and successes, self-worth, past experiences, and exposure to various behaviors and situations such as poverty, discrimination, and love. Your perception is also affected by nervous system functions that must be acknowledged or the *why* of behavior might never be realized.

The environment is a key consideration in this entire process because all the stuff in our child's world will affect every single part of the system and ultimately behavior. The environment refers to many things:

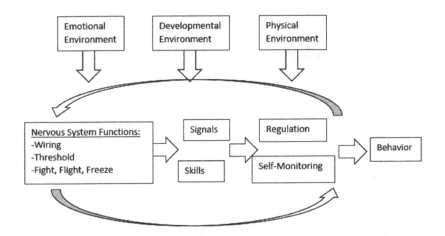

- Behavior is affected by our emotional environment. If a child feels supported, behavior will be different. If there is abuse or poverty, this creates an environment that clearly impacts *everything*.
- Developmental environment takes into consideration 'in utero' or early childhood occurrences. A difficult pregnancy, exposure to drugs or alcohol during pregnancy and even factors related to birth can affect the system at any point.

- There is also the immediate physical environment that can alter behavior. We can use strategies and tools to change this physical environment and ideas for this will be included in these pages.

Examine the reason you are reading this book... your child and the struggle. Who is this child? What is their personality, and how does this contribute to their struggle? Can you relate to them? Do you ever use words like lazy, defiant, or disrespectful when you describe their behavior? Further explanation will review concepts related to:

- Wiring- Who is your child? This is innate and similar to personality. We can't change their wiring but we must be aware of it because it will affect how your child is responding. Wiring is going to affect what a child is drawn to. This determines development, helps with signals and affects all behavior. Strategies won't affect wiring. Wiring will affect what strategies need to be used and will explain the signals that affect behavior.

- Self-monitoring- Can your child identify when things feel off? If a child can sense what is going on inside, they can generally adapt and feel better. When they don't know what they are feeling or don't have words to describe these feelings, they won't be able to adjust their behavior, ask for help, or regulate.

- Regulation- Regulation is the ability to feel good even when things aren't perfect. It is the cornerstone of finding Happy.

- Threshold- How does your child generally respond? This is driven by wiring, but it can fluctuate. Do they need more excitement or a quieter space? Some days they will need one more than the other. Some environments will affect how much they can handle. The threshold will be affected by strategies so it is critical to understand.

- Fight, Flight, or Freeze- This is the nervous system function of protection. When this mechanism is triggered, it is impossible to control behavior, learn or regulate. Your child's wiring and threshold for input will determine when this occurs and how they will respond. Some tend to fight, while others might be more prone to flight.

Two big puzzle pieces that affect every behavior we encounter are related to 1) signals to the brain and 2) skills the brain uses to respond. If there is a breakdown in either, there will be a problem. For now, and to simplify much of the picture, just knowing what signals and skills are is a start because this is ultimately how we find balance and feel good.

- *Signals* come from sensory processing inside our body to tell us how we are doing: are we hungry, thirsty, tired, overwhelmed, too hot, in pain, etc. Signals can also be transmitted relative to what is going on outside. This can include the pace of the world, too much noise, and also the good stuff. These signals go to the thinking brain for a response. Our brain learns with every signal that comes in. If there are too many signals, the brain gets bombarded and overwhelmed and can't learn. If there aren't enough signals, the brain doesn't have sufficient input telling it what is going on. These are both problems. As a parent dealing with behavior, figuring out if the signals are working is critical because signals communicate how everything is going.
- *Skills* become effectual when the brain can analyze, process, respond, and learn, but this only happens if the signals make their way to the thinking part of the brain. The skills are related to executive functioning, and they are developmental, which means they improve with practice and over time. If you push too hard before they are developed, you will see frustration, poor behavior, and lots of failures.

Looking at your own system helps you better understand your child's system. Your nervous system functions, your environmental factors, and how signals and skills work in *your* system are all relevant because this affects how you look at absolutely *everything*.

- Think about your world, the people in it, and your own experiences that molded your perception and judgement of the behavior you are watching.
- Who are you? How do you see your child based on where you came from and the experiences or emotions you felt growing up?
- How did your parents approach issues, and did it work? Are you parenting in a similar way?
- Consider who you are parenting with. What are they like? Are they helpful?
- What are your stressors? How do you manage them? Does it work?

When you understand all the pieces of the puzzle that go into behavior, you can begin to look at this behavior through a different lens. Now your response may be different, and hopefully the outcome will be too. When you acknowledge who your child is innately (their wiring), and begin to recognize what they can and can't handle (their threshold), the  cause of behavior becomes a little more transparent, and the puzzle becomes easier to solve. You might even discover some things about yourself in the process which might explain some of the circumstances in your world. Some of these discoveries help the puzzle pieces fit, and some make it really challenging. When the pieces aren't fitting and life is hard, what then? How can you make them fit? How can you explain what is causing the behavior you are seeing? All of this is possible with a little different perspective.

You are going to get a glimpse into who I am through reading the words in this book because it is about me, my journey and my experiences as a therapist and a parent. In my twenty years as an occupational therapist, I have worked with hundreds of children both in school and through my private practice. I have researched and applied information from other experts with different ideas and theories. All of this has increased my knowledge of children and the nervous system functions that affect how they behave, engage and survive. Through all this, I keep coming back to the same concepts. My professional and personal journey taught me things I could not have learned in school and it is these concepts I share with you.

A LITTLE BIT ABOUT ME

My name is Kristin.
I was born Martinsen and married Andrew Robison.
I have two incredible kids, Jens and Annika.
We have a standard poodle, two cats, and a hedgehog
I got in a moment of poor judgment
that turned into a very cool experience.

When I was in college, I was in a car accident that changed everything about who I thought I would be. I guess I was mad, I was certainly bummed, but I think I was mad because I didn't understand why this had happened to *me*. Eventually, I decided I didn't want to be mad at the world anymore for what happened. I didn't like how that anger made me feel.

At this moment, I realized that I had power and control over *one thing*... how I respond. I had to find purpose, and possibly goodness, in what happened. This experience helped me to understand who I am. I had to redefine. I was an athlete, but now everything I did hurt. I was a student, but just sitting to study was miserable.

I had no idea this accident would so significantly impact who I am as a human, and ultimately as a therapist. In many ways it was a gift, because in every negative I was forced to find the positive... the purpose. I was my own first therapist of sorts, and not only for Occupational Therapy.

Fast forward ...

My son was born, and he was perfect. He didn't sleep; he cried for the first nine months and had reflux so bad that everything smelled like rotten milk. But he was alert, inquisitive, engaged, engaging, and positively perfect. His smile would light up a room. He asked questions about everything and loved anything related to dinosaurs, Legos, and science. School should have been fun, right? Except it wasn't. As bright and engaging as he was, he could not play school. He would get so excited by the content that he wouldn't bother to do the homework or worksheets.

I had no idea how to help this child. My child. He knew he was different, that he couldn't focus, that school was *not* fun. I had to adapt to help my own son because despite having had therapy from the day he was born, he still struggled. Sensory processing is what I knew as an occupational therapist. But there was more going on.

Fast forward again... Brain tumor.

This one shook me, and there was no way I could have prepared for this. How could this be the end? How could *anything* positive come out of this one? My son was eleven, my daughter eight. My tumor was benign, but it took over a year to feel relatively normal after treatment. What I realized next was incredible... this tumor didn't make me mad. This tumor was a gift because it made me realize that what I had figured out needed to be written down, for my kids and for others who haven't figured out how to help their child.

My son needed a way to figure out what he felt inside, but first he needed the words and a way to learn to express them. The Dragon Phenomenon was born out of this need. Once he had the words, we could find the tools to help with his signals so he could focus and feel good inside. I also realized my daughter needed these words too, but for very different reasons.

What I do as a therapist doesn't fall into just one professional wheelhouse. It also doesn't just apply to kids like mine. Each individual is unique with different strengths and challenges, and the key to figuring out how to find Happy is understanding the many puzzle pieces that go into behavior. I will introduce you to the dragon concept because it is a great way to discuss the various signals that tell our brain what to do. Dragons help kids explain what they are feeling and guide them toward the "*what now?*"

Fast forward... now my son is in middle school.

Smart kid, terrible grades. Why? He understood the content but forgot to hand in his work. He hated to write, so the content he was supposed to study wasn't on the page when he got home. The missing assignments piled up, but letting him fall on his face wasn't working because he couldn't dig himself out of the giant hole he was in.

What people don't realize is that kids will find success if they *can*. If they aren't turning in work or aren't doing what they are told, it is usually because they *can't*. Not because they *won't or don't want to*. Wouldn't you choose success over failure if both were viable options? Executive functioning is something that had to be considered. My process had to look at the whole picture which now included signals and skills.

Today I give classes to parents and teachers to help them figure out *why* kids can't find success. I consult in my private practice with families who just need to know their child is okay. I talk to people every day about "this" child. This child who is smart but not working to their potential. This child who might not be able to handle anything emotionally. This child who can't find their smile at the end of the day… and frankly neither can their parents. Any adult who lives with this child knows the heartache this kid feels when success is nowhere in sight. Some give up because it is just too hard. And this doesn't only affect kids! Adults give up too when they never find success, and this destroys self-esteem, self-worth, and completely undermines any hope for social-emotional health.

This book is my hope that every child can find their smile at the end of the day.

One day my friend and I were talking about her son and she shared with me the incredible emotions that she wrote as she watched her son in a therapy session. Writing was her way to cope and push through the pain. You may feel the pain as you read the emotion in her words; it is so raw and real. Her words introduce this book if only to show that we are not in this alone and neither are our kids.

A MOTHER'S ACCOUNT OF HER SON'S THERAPY SESSION

COMPOSED AND CONTRIBUTED WITH PERMISSION BY CARLY SYNDERGAARD

Truth…

No matter how hard I try, I make mistakes
A. Always
B. Often
C. Sometimes
D. Never

"Always" he said

Other kids are just better than I am. I'm not as good.
A. Always
B. Often
C. Sometimes
D. Never

He hesitated and cast a quick glance toward me, then quickly back down.
"Always" he said quietly
A tear slipped silently down my cheek.
He handed me a tissue.
He always does.

It hurts him when I cry.

He has that kind of a heart.

So aware, so thoughtful, so much desire to do good. Be good.

And so small.

He always looks so small sitting on that couch.

Quiet and attentive and willing.

It makes me wonder why anyone would bring him here.

Except I do.

I bring him.

In those moments it's hard for me to remember the frustration, anger and tears he has caused me when he is not this boy.

But it's not really hard.

I always remember.

It rides under the surface of my consciousness like a small wave of anxiety I try to ignore.

Then crashes into the shores and whips my feet out from under me like the flip of a switch.

He shuts down.

Closes off.

When the fight gets too exhausting, he stops trying.

"I don't care" he yells

A dagger from the mouth of the most caring boy I know.

He looks so small.

Because he is.

He is too small to fight this fight alone.

To battle his own brain.

His frustration and anger push me away and his soul grasps at me and begs me to stay.

And in a breath it's over.

His heart is so heavy.

His apologies sincerely pure.

Heartbreakingly pure.

Pain is something you walk around with under your clothes.
You hold it close and tuck it deep in hopes no one will notice it poking out.
It's embarrassing.
It hurts.
When it's your own its unbearably heavy.
When it's your child it's suffocating.
Shame and judgment your constant companions.

People are good.
I truly believe that.
Unintentionally they poke at the pain.
It's not their fault.
The nerves are exposed.
Everywhere I look there are borderline genius children.
Everywhere.
Parents proudly stating how advanced their kids are.
Calls home.
"Too smart"
"Best kid in the class"
"I can't keep him/her busy enough"
"School is so easy"
"Reading 3 grade levels ahead"
"Math whiz"

You smile.
Because it's a happy thing.
You smile.
And wonder if there is anyone else in the world that feels like you.
That feels like they are barely holding it together.
That doesn't get phone calls home like that.
That prays the phone doesn't ring from school.
Anyone else whose heart drops when it does.
Anyone who is brought to their knees in frustrating wonder about how long it will be so hard.

Anyone else that feels it is hard.
Anyone who scans the room and wonders how everyone seems to
have this mothering thing figured out
Anyone that feels like a failure.

The diagnosis came gently. With a quiet smile full of hope.
I love her for this.
ADHD rarely travels alone.
It usually hides something under the surface.
For him it was a mood disorder.
A form of childhood depression.
Which is common in our family history but not in him.

I feel sad.
  A. Always
  B. Often
  C. Sometimes
  D. Never

"Almost never" he said.
I wasn't surprised.
I would have said the same thing.

"Childhood depression is manifested as irritability" she said
"A mood disorder is not the same thing as adult depression as we
know it"
An education I would have not chosen, yet I seemed to have been
enrolled in.
I would have picked forestry.

So I coach.
And coach.
And coach.
All the coping mechanisms we have learned.
I guide him with almost perfect patience.

Until I don't.
Because patience is exhausting.
So I start over.
And so does he.
Because I mirror this great truth to him.
You can always start over.
You can always get up and try again.
You can always do better.
Be better.
Some struggles are hard for you and easy for others but it is no less possible.
Trying matters.

I have to do this.
I have to love him.
Because he happens to own my heart.
And he is so small.
And so good.

PARENTING TODAY

Why do kids do what they do? How do they always manage to embrace joy, even after an epic meltdown? When my son came into my world, it suddenly became 150% more intense. The mother bear syndrome I had seen in many meetings at school with parents was now my reality. Quickly, I could see that I was on a life-altering journey... for everyone involved!

Parenting is not at all what I thought it would be. I had a plan. There would be consistency, hugs every day, no sugar, healthy food and no need to say "no" because when you explain the *why* they won't do it again. All those lovely ideas you formulated when you discovered parenthood was in your future all seemed so realistic. Some of it worked, like the hugging part. But honestly, the rest was a day-to-day game of survival, and survival is something you get very good at as a parent. The many parents I meet in my office are doing just that.

Today's generation of children faces many challenges that we parents never experienced at such a young age and this skews our perspective. Things we played with as kids are everyday devices used in school and work today. For the most part, our kids don't know a world without instant messages, information at your fingertips in an instant, and opportunity *everywhere*. When I ask my son to mow the lawn, he negotiates and eventually proclaims that cutting the grass isn't going to make him more successful. He went on to inform me that there are people who play games for a living, and that is their work. Did you know you can have a YouTube channel dedicated to gaming and actually make money? He had no trouble seeing that this was work, but I had a really hard time because of my past experiences. If you are playing a game on a computer, that is *playing* not work.

How do we navigate the world today, especially as parents? How can we possibly instill knowledge and wisdom in our children when they believe they can play online games all day and earn a living? What was important for my generation to survive doesn't completely apply to kids today because the world is so different. Perhaps today our values need another look. What I want for my child is what my parents wanted for me, but is there a different way to achieve this based on what's available to children today?

Are we capable of understanding, and maybe even respecting the way our children are navigating and learning in their academic world? I know my perspective has changed through the course of seeing what my children can do with all this technology at their disposal. It's all so easy, and wow, the job got done and fast. How can this be possible?

Yes, parents have a difficult job today. Children appear to have it so easy, but with all this incredible technology and speed comes another issue that's cropping up in all kinds of kids. Gifted, high performing, typical learners, and those with learning disabilities are all affected by our world and the speed that it is flying by. The pace is what seems to be hard. Kids are missing the cues. They aren't catching all the steps. They're not learning to read the room anymore, so we must adjust our expectations and find the just-right challenge, or they won't know *how* to find success.

CHILD DEVELOPMENT

I have always liked the brick wall analogy when discussing child development. A child is born and comes into the world wired a certain way, but when they are exposed to different things, another layer of bricks goes on the wall. When babies are lying on their tummies for instance, they can see their hand and feel pressure on their stomach, chest, and legs.

- They move their hand and watch it as it moves… important for later reading skills.
- They kick their feet or arch up and can suddenly move across the floor or roll over… important for motor planning and coordination.
- They engage other humans like in the store vs. watching a video on the iPad… important for future social skills and the executive skill of reading the room.
- They feel the softness of the carpet or the hard, cold floor and soon learn that what they do affects how things feel… important for cause and effect and later learning.
- They reach for an object and now have a foundation for where their hand is in space… important for later writing and sports.

Foundational bricks are being formed! Much of this simple, almost boring activity is creating a critical foundation for further learning. This foundation affects their brain and the internal signals that they depend on for regulation.

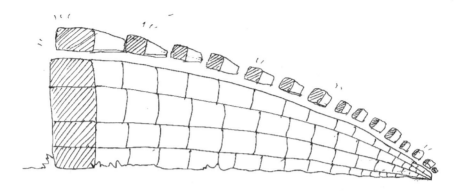

Now, imagine a child is sitting upright in a bouncy seat and watching a developmentally appropriate television show or movie. Trust me, I did it too! I remember quickly switching our satellite television programming to include as many baby or child-based educational shows as possible. It was a fabulous solution to the daily meltdown at 5:30 p.m. But consider the experience this child is having compared to the child on the floor, entertaining themselves.

Babies don't walk or sit up immediately on their own for a reason. My new found solution of television now meant my baby's visual system was being hit very early, with a lot of input that they wouldn't have otherwise been exposed to on their own because of where they were developmentally. But this TV stuff was exciting, and my son loved it! Why would he lie around, trying to get his big toe in his mouth, when he could watch cute figures move across the screen while swinging in his new baby seat? That toe and mouth game suddenly seems boring and uneventful! Technology is impressive, but sadly, it can replace activities that are fundamentally important for the development of more complex skills.

As kids get bigger and begin to move around in their world, it can be hard to practice moderation with technology. Cool toys, movies, play equipment, and robotic options keep our kids occupied, but we can forget the importance of simply letting them *find* something to do. Computers, phones, and portable movies are sometimes too readily used as a babysitter or behavior management system. This can result in foundational skills, social skills, and executive functioning skills not developing as we would expect and this affects the integrity of their wall.

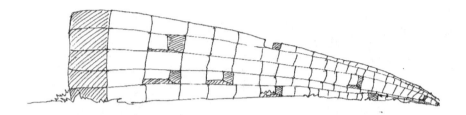

Brain development must be pivotal in our expectations and how we program our academics. We've seen drastic changes in human behavior and determined different ways to test and evaluate our kids, but we've been unable to adapt, as a system, to meet all of the *needs* of our child. We have a pretty archaic educational system that hasn't evolved with our kids, despite technological advances. Not all kids are college-bound, but sometimes we expect them to all be on the same course and exposed to the same stuff in school. This can be a huge reason why we see some of the perceived negative behaviors and this is related to child development.

People always ask why kids today seem to struggle more than they did twenty years ago. Today there is more information and research about issues that severely impact behavior and regulation. Perhaps this added knowledge allows us to identify behaviors we have always seen, but didn't know how to label. Maybe people with poor behavior are not written off so quickly now.

While knowledge helps with understanding, consider also what play looks like today. What do kids do in their free time? Video games and computers are even in schools now and required for most assignments. I don't mean to give technology a totally bad rap, and there are positive skills that develop with its use. Have you seen the game Minecraft? My child can navigate that world so fast it makes my head spin to watch. Pretty impressive spatial mapping, yes. Applicable to real life? Probably. What was I doing in my free time at their age? I was biking through the neighborhood, building forts, inventing goofy games with evolving rules. My nervous system and brain were receiving input from all my senses with these different activities. I could handle more information because my nervous system was getting so much input while I played. This is very different than what I'm watching my child do right now. Technology has presented an incredible opportunity, but it also replaces much of the active outside play that was happening twenty years ago. Our nervous system molds according to our experiences, and experience is very different for children today.

SCREEN TIME VS. OUTSIDE TIME IS AFFECTING THE WORLD OUR CHILDREN ARE EXPERIENCING, WHICH IN TURN INFLUENCES THE KIND OF INPUT THEIR NERVOUS SYSTEM WILL BUILD ON FOR FURTHER DEVELOPMENT.

When skills come in and signals are working, developmental milestones *will* happen.

If we push too fast or too soon, we will see problems... if not now, eventually.

Reading out of a book might be a skill that the eyes and brain are not yet developmentally prepared for. A child may get pretty good at faking it when these skills are not developed. Effective visual scanning needs to be practiced at a pace that allows for it to mature or it will affect math and reading. Faking it will affect that developmental wall!

- When you move your body, endorphins are released that make you feel energetic, motivated, and happy.
- Your brain is sending and receiving signals that help you keep track of precisely what your body is doing, where it is in space, and plan other motor skills. Foundational skills are all at work. The vestibular, proprioceptive, and tactile systems will be discussed soon because they affect play and how it impacts regulation.

- The more signals our brain sends and receives, the more efficient the synapses within the brain become for later learning. You can prepare your brain to learn with movement.
- The more senses used during play and learning (touch, smell, sight, hearing, taste, and movement sensations), the easier it is for our brain to store and retrieve information quickly. It is incredible how different senses affect memory. For instance, when I smell roses and Aqua Net hairspray, I remember historic details I would never have thought of related to being with my grama. The storage and retrieval of these memories are linked to this smell.

Knowledge is key because it changes the way you look at your child. Next, you will need strategies and tools because these will help your child begin to change that behavior from the inside out. Creating strategies should involve the sensory system and foundations of development such as what it was like in-utero. Dark, warm, wet, and confining are sensations we want to use first. The outside world is clearly very different. Bright, loud, and varying temperature can often be stressful. It is easy to see how kids and babies can easily overstimulate. Try returning to the basics and how your child could be soothed as a baby, and incorporate the things that calmed them when they were stressed or upset. If they loved a pacifier or sucking on their thumb, find something for them to suck or chew on. Maybe they loved to be swaddled. Now you know they might like a weighted blanket or to play games with heavy pressure. Here is a list of ideas that can be fun ways to start. Don't forget to involve your child in this process too, because sometimes they know exactly what feels good and what *doesn't*.

STRATEGIES THAT ALIGN WITH
CHILD DEVELOPMENT

- Try a warm bath with dim lighting. Use a night light, battery-operated candles or a couple of glow-sticks in the water. They can fish for them or hook them together to make shapes to allow for less intense light.

- Make a fort that can be completely dark and is quiet. Entryway closets are the best! Help your child make the fort with pillows or stuffed animals, and any other comforting items. You can use a dim flashlight or glow-stick if they are afraid of the dark. The goal is to allow the brain just to have a break. We want this space dark and quiet, but we don't want them scared. Encouraging your child's imagination in the building process allows them to come up with things that help them feel better but also gives them control over things they don't like. These problems can now be solved before the emotion of fear arises. When kids feel like they have some control, they have more buy-in. If you have a child who isn't afraid of the dark, have it completely dark. If they are hesitant, try going in with them even for just five minutes with complete darkness… it will make you feel better too! After a stressful day of holding it together, they have a safe place that allows all their senses to have a break.

- Deep pressure is very organizing for everyone. Even people who don't like to be touched can usually tolerate deep pressure as opposed to light touch.

- Hammocks, especially those that are made of neoprene, provide a safe cocoon-type experience that can allow them to decompress from their day.

- Deep massage with oil provides the organizing input of deep pressure and when paired with darkness, can be invigorating.

- Games that involve deep pressure give input with the added bonus of fun. Play a game of taco stand where the child gets wrapped up in a blanket like a burrito and then add the condiments such as pillows to mimic adding the salsa, cheese, olives, etc. You can also make a burger with the couch cushions as the bun and add ketchup, mustard, etc. Push down hard and slow for calming input, or quick and hard for alerting input.

- Return to the basics. Good old-fashioned advice like "go out and play" is critical because play is the primary job of a child. In this ever-changing world where our kids are doing more work in their elementary years than we did in all of high school, our children need to play more than ever. Play allows the body and brain to work together. When children are left to their own resources for play, amazing things happen. They begin to come up with ideas which they test out or talk out with friends or siblings. These ideas evolve, are tried, changed, and discussed… sounds a bit like learning to me!

- Linear rocking is a forward and backward motion that is calming and provides added input without increasing the stress level. Try a rocking chair, swing, or even sitting with your child in your lap and rocking.

- Going back to basics is foundational for higher learning. Children today are pushed to read and write at earlier ages, even before they are developmentally ready. In doing this, we can be creating learning issues that show up down the road.

- When children make block figures or create playdough letters, they develop spatial skills and fine motor dexterity for writing, cutting, tying shoes, etc.

- When they throw objects at a target, they are developing visual motor skills that help advance reading skills and copying notes from the board.

- When they are bored and have to come up with games, they are developing executive skills.

- Tummy time, tummy time, tummy time. It doesn't matter what age! Extension of the neck (see photo below) is very alerting for the nervous system. If your child is sick of reading or homework, have them lie on their tummy; they will get neck extension, which can help them focus. They are putting weight into their arms, elbows, and shoulders, which will help with foundational strength and stability for writing. *And* it is different, so it might even be fun.

WIRING

HOW IT AFFECTS YOUR CHILD'S SIGNALS

The one thing I discovered, both as a parent and as a therapist working with parents, is the more you understand your child, the easier it is to parent. Since we have no instruction book, this is all I could surmise. You need to understand your own wiring first because this affects how you see your child and react as a parent. Next you will start the process of learning about your child's wiring.

Personality can be referred to as "wiring" and when things are hard-wired, they aren't going to change. We don't want to change our child's personality, we just want to change how well their wiring works in different situations. If this child is wired talkative and busy, how can they find success in the library or in the movies? When our child's personality isn't working for a certain activity, is there something we can do to help them find success?

I use the analogy of a toy when talking about wiring. Think about a toy bunny that jumps fast when you put in the battery. This toy is wired to jump and go fast. This is not to say that if you make it jump up a steep hill, it is still going to go fast, but in the end, this bunny is all about jumping and speed.

Now think about a turtle. Put that battery in and guess what? There will be no jumping and very little will happen quickly because it isn't wired for speed, it is wired for this slower pace. If I were to put this toy turtle at the top of a steep decline and let it go, it will likely go faster, but it will never jump or go at the pace of the bunny.

This is wiring.

I knew each one of my children would be vastly different from the other even before they were born. When I was pregnant with my son, he constantly moved with strength and vigor. My daughter was rolling gracefully every few hours. Suffice it to say, this is how they are today. Understanding that my son was a mover helped me to come up with activities and ideas that would support his wiring. My daughter needed a quieter space with less intensity and still does to this day.

One of the first steps, aside from learning about your child and their wiring, is to help them understand it too. You can do therapy with a child every day for a year, and at the end of that year, you won't have changed this child's wiring. You can affect their skill level, performance, and overall awareness, but they will maintain that same energy, or wiring, no matter what you do. Knowing this and sharing this with your child is the most critical first step to helping them become happy, successful, realistic, independent individuals who are comfortable in their own skin regardless of the setting. Acknowledging, respecting, and adjusting to your child's wiring will help you in your relationship with your child. Sometimes all it takes to change an entire family dynamic is awareness.

It is humbling to admit we are simply a guide for our child.

Their successes and failures are theirs.

How can we be a good guide without making their journey a reflection of who *we* are?

So how do we do this? Go through these questions about your child. As you do, use some self-reflection to see if you can find similarities or differences between you and your child. This awareness may expose the most obvious reason you can't find a way to help them. Maybe you're too alike and you don't want them to go through what you did. Or you are so different it seems like their behavior is more a choice than who they actually are.

1. Are they movers or more mellow?

2. Do they thrive on attention or enjoy being solo?
3. Are they observing or jumping in?
4. How do they wake up? Happy, crabby, quiet?
5. Do they go to bed easily?
6. Are they always talking? Did they start talking early? Do their siblings do all the talking?
7. Do they prefer a quiet, calm space, or do better with lots going on?
8. Do they need things a little slower? Maybe they require more time to process.

These are only a few questions that help you recognize your child's wiring. Another easy, child-friendly way to determine wiring is through the childhood stories of Christopher Robin by A.A. Milne. Would you call your child more Tigger, Pooh, or Eeyore? Sounds silly I know, but I always smile when I think of my Tigger-like child.

A lot goes into the analysis of wiring. Do you see any trends in behavior? Do they always do the same thing? Can you figure out what came before or after the behavior? Is this behavior more than wiring and something that might need to be addressed? Is it something that can change?

Talking to my son about his wiring opened lots of room for questions.

- Why can other kids focus, and I can't?
- I have trouble starting anything… does that mean I am lazy even though I try really hard?
- Why, if I'm smart, is this so hard?
- Why does my stomach hurt all the time?

I now knew part of the puzzle. He is wired busy. He needs to exercise before big tests or in the middle of the day. He needs to drink water and have noise, music, YouTube or car races on when he's studying. He's a talker. He needs to have all his stuff ready and cleared out when he sits down to study because he gets distracted too easily. His wiring is nothing to be embarrassed about because it is what it is. He is an out-of-the-box kid, and a true wonder and delight because of this!

But how can I help him reconcile this kind of wiring in himself when he's only seeing the struggle, especially in school? How can I help reconcile this in *me?* Why do I feel his wiring might be embarrassing? Is it because it is not what society deems as "normal"? Many kids today are slipping through the cracks. Maybe they always have. All I know is that unless we change our perception and stop expecting everyone to be "normal", we will never help these kids, or people in general, find their true path.

We talked some more.

- We talked about what is problematic in his world.
- We talked about what he loves about his world.
- We talked about ideas, strategies, and times of the day that were tough, and others that were easy.
- We talked about teachers and how their various personalities, or *their* wiring, affected him in school.
- We talked about things that motivated him, and what made it hard to focus. After all, it is his system and *he is the expert*. I had to frequently remind myself that I was simply a *guide*. He had to figure it out. He had to understand.
- I shared *my* wiring and determined it was pretty similar to his in some ways. We talked about what I learned growing up, and he shared his thoughts with me.
- We talked about his dad's wiring and the fact that it is very different than his. This could make it hard for the two of them to relate at times.

Don't think for a moment I had this figured out. No way! The moment you think you've got it, something else crops up. I dove into more research. I needed strategies not only for him, but for the many other misunderstood kids I was trying to help at work. I talked with parents to help them understand how their child was wired, and how sensory processing and executive functioning might affect a certain situation *because* of their wiring. I realized that some kinds of wiring don't mesh well with others and that the chemistry between a parent or teacher and a child can be critical for the success and self-esteem of that child.

My son began to understand that who he is and how he's wired explains his view of the world, the people in his world, and how he feels about all of it. This kid thinks outside the box, and while his amazing personality and the energy that comes with it is contagious and incredible, it also makes life more challenging at times. His wiring determines the strategies that work for him and when he needs to use them. He didn't need to change *who* he is… he should be proud of who he is. But life isn't always geared for his type of wiring; he needed to change how he did *some* things so he could adapt when things got hard.

He also learned that he has some control over this situation.

I'm sure life would be easier if all kids, people, could just fit into *that* box.

But some don't.

I don't know that I want them to either, because it would be boring if everyone fit in the same box. I do want to figure out how to help these out-of-the-box kids "play" school, work or life. Maybe we can encourage them to find a path that allows them to use their talents in a productive, quality of life  way that might open many more boxes with beautiful shapes for others to explore.

My son is usually like Tigger... the more bouncing the better, and always a smile on his face. He always has to be in front of his sister when we hike. He wants to do what he wants vs. following instructions. He jumps right in and hates preparation. Me too, so I can tell my wiring is similar to his because this is exactly what I do!

If I try to change his wiring, I will simply push him away and squash his beautiful energy. This is especially true if he goes against who he is because he feels like he needs to please me. He won't be able to talk to me honestly if I can't be honest about who he is and fully respect and cherish him. I love his energy... everyone is drawn to his energy, but when it comes time to sit down and do homework or sit quietly in class and listen vs. talking to a peer about a new invention, the challenges begin.

School gets harder every year. Children who are bright can usually fly by the seat of their pants for a while. Usually around third grade, things get harder to pretend and life gets really difficult.

No more smiles, lots more bouncing.

I was lucky. My son had so many amazing teachers who completely embraced his wiring and out-of-the-box thinking. They were willing to look at him through a different lens. I didn't realize how much I needed this as a parent... I just needed to know that someone finally understood my child. When an adult in a child's life doesn't understand or isn't willing to see behavior in a different way, it can be really hard on everyone.

REGULATION AND SELF-MONITORING

Regulation is the ability to function even when things aren't perfect. To function like this, we need to be able to monitor our signals. When self-monitoring occurs, it allows for regulation because we now know that something is off, or doesn't feel right. Self-monitoring and regulation are big pieces of the puzzle for behavior because they allow for communication to occur.

- Self-monitoring is the ability to monitor signals and then communicate the findings between the body and the brain.
- Regulation is what happens when self-monitoring occurs and we can adjust. Behavior communicates whether regulation is occurring or not. If someone is laughing, we know they are happy and regulated. When they are crying, they need help. If we know what is off, we can often adjust and adapt. We must have some sort of indication that there is a problem or we won't know that this child needs help.

When kids are young and don't yet have words, we depend on their behavior to tell us what they need. But what if we can't make sense of their behavior? This usually ends in a tantrum or meltdown that is irrational, loud, and virtually impossible to navigate gracefully. When kids are little, we expect that these tantrums will occur because they are too young to know why things don't feel right, or how to communicate this with us. We search for hints in their behavior.

Sometimes when kids are older and able to communicate, they don't. We have come to expect words to better understand their needs, so we hope for fewer tantrums. But regulation is completely irrelevant of age or the ability to communicate. These older and smarter kids should just automatically regulate... right? This is where things can get tricky.

If you don't know why the math homework is so hard, even though it was no problem this morning at school, you won't know how to help. The math skills are there, but the regulation is not. Maybe they forgot to get a snack after school and are hungry. Maybe it is hard to focus after a long day at school or maybe their best friend being mad about something at lunch is where their mind is, not on math.

Regulation and self-monitoring are affected by signals and skills. Regulation helps us control behavior, but it is completely dependent on self-monitoring.

SELF-MONITORING

The ability to sense what is going on inside. Knowing when something is off gives you awareness that affects your behavior

REGULATION

The ability to function even when things aren't perfect

Two major things that will affect how we self-monitor and then how we can regulate our behavior are sensory processing and executive functioning.

- <u>Sensory processing</u> depends on the signals coming into our system. This information from our world and inside our body creates a signal in order for our brain to learn or respond. Signals are incredibly important to monitor because if the nervous system doesn't pick up signals, there will be no reason to adjust. If too many signals come in, nothing will make sense, and there will be no adjustment and likely no appropriate response.

- <u>Executive functioning</u> drives the skills that are behind our behavior. They are skills that develop in the brain, and they are responsible for many important things related to behavior. If the skills aren't mature yet, it will be difficult to behave and find success. If you can read the room, then you can adjust your behavior to be more appropriate and you will more easily find Happy. If you can think before you talk, you can keep friends, laugh, and not hurt feelings. All of this is required for Happy.

SELF-MONITORING

The first real step to regulation is knowing something is off. If you aren't aware that your tank is out of gas, you won't know why the car won't start. This is self-monitoring.

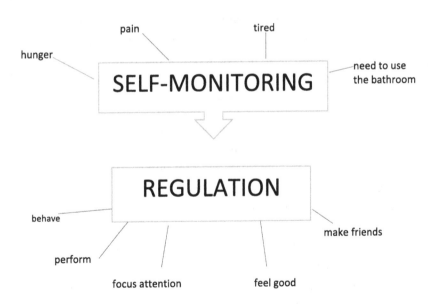

Self-monitoring is not easy and many adults haven't mastered this either. When self-monitoring doesn't happen, conflict follows. You must know what is wrong in order to communicate, respond, or adjust behavior.

- If I can self-monitor, chances are this will help me regulate because now I know the *why* of how I feel.
- If I can then solve that problem and figure out what I need to be successful, I can successfully regulate my behavior.
- If I can communicate this to someone, they can help me regulate the behavior that I can't.

The problem with certain types of wiring or various conditions that affect behavior is that self-monitoring is essentially not happening. If the sensations within the body are not the typical, "I need to use the bathroom" or "I'm hungry, tired, sick or thirsty," then how does this child communicate what is wrong? Do they even know words to describe these feelings? In many cases there are no words, and tantrums and behavioral regulation issues become a daily occurrence. Older children who have seemingly good communication skills may struggle with this as well.

> Sadly, negative behavior or tantrums are also what begin to define your child. Suddenly the sweet, curious, funny child you know so well, is replaced by one that is moody, whiny and essentially uncomfortable in their own skin.

Sometimes brain development isn't at the same level as age or intelligence. If the skills of planning, starting, staying focused, or turning off a bad mood aren't fully mature, behavior will be affected. When kids are wired in atypical ways and they can't figure out what they are experiencing, the process of planning, starting, or staying focused can't occur because they don't even know there is a problem. When kids have difficulty processing sensory information from their world or their body, this can be a big stumbling block. Not only can they not figure out *what* is wrong, they have no idea how to get your help in figuring it out. It won't matter how many words your child can say if they can't figure out *what* is wrong. If they can't self-monitor, there is no way they can self-regulate.

One of the best ways to weed out what is going on inside is through body scans. Imagine holding a magic wand.

Start at the top of your head and move slowly down the body, paying attention to every part the wand moves over.

- Maybe your head hurts, or your eyes are blurry.
- Are you thirsty or hungry?
- Next is the chest. Is your heart racing or pounding? How is breathing... slow or fast?
- Then the belly. The belly has a lot to focus on because it can be upset, hungry, have butterflies, be too full, tell you to use the bathroom, etc.
- Legs and knees are next... toes, and so on.

Go slowly and focus on each part as it passes under this magic wand. If your child is older, have them visualize or focus on each part of their body from top to bottom until they figure out *what* they feel, or at least *where* they feel it. This is a great activity to use when your child is *not* upset. If they can get good at this strategy *before* they are uncomfortable it will provide information that will be more effective when they are upset.

Fight, flight, or freeze is a nervous system response referred to as survival mode. We can't logically use our brain in the moment of distress because we are protecting ourselves through fighting, freezing, or running. This is why scans help. They allow us to figure out strategies *before* getting upset and going into this mode.

Nothing can happen if we can't regulate. When we don't feel good in our own skin, we can't play anything... not school, not games, not life. Regulation is dependent on many things, so this is where the bulk of content begins. The *why* of behavior will always revolve around regulation. If your car doesn't have gas, it won't run. If we can't regulate, we can't function... anywhere.

Regulation can be challenging, especially for young children, and it is dependent upon the ability to self-monitor. If I can stop for a moment when I feel agitated, I can figure out that I might be hungry. This is self-monitoring, and it is a critical prerequisite to being able to regulate.

I NEED THE ABILITY TO:

1. **STOP**
2. **REFLECT**
3. **PROBLEM SOLVE**

BEHAVIOR ISN'T GETTING BETTER, BUT WHY?

Have you ever had those moments where you're moving fast or on the go, only to come inside and find that you're practically yelling? Your nervous system is still in "go mode". Adjusting it to a new, quiet environment can take some work. We know the body needs to send signals to the brain to get moving and to slow down. Sometimes a strategy can make a behavior worse. This is an out-of-sync strategy. Many kids have trouble getting their nervous system where it needs to be for the expectations in their world.

I remember as a new therapist, I was helping a very dysregulated child and decided we would run on the track to make him feel better and improve his focus ability. I knew he was a mover and thought this would be perfect! I had a hard time getting him out there at all, but then after he ran and ran, he was actually less regulated than when we started. Certain strategies don't work for some kids because their nervous system won't turn off or adjust with certain types of input. Running, or vestibular input, made things worse for this kid because now his system was operating even higher and still wouldn't come down! I assumed running would work because this is a kid wired for busy, but after seeing his response, I knew he needed help adjusting. I changed gears, and we did some pushups, carried some heavy equipment to the office, and sat with a weighted blanket to breathe before trying to return to math. I was able to help this child regulate by using a different root... the proprioceptive root. Talk about an "aha" moment! I learned that some strategies could make things worse sometimes, and we both realized that his system needed heavy, calming, controlled proprioceptive input, not vestibular and not running! If something doesn't work the first time, try something different. Don't keep pushing with something that isn't effective.

Another piece of critical information has to do with *when* we utilize strategies. Many of the strategies that kids need must occur *before work* can happen. When a child needs input to respond, but we use strategies as rewards for work, behavior does not improve. If you put a reward out there but your child doesn't respond, you need to consider the *why*. If your child is wiggling around and struggling to do homework and you offer the yoga ball to sit on during TV time *after* they get their homework done, certainly they would do their homework, right? But if their system needs the movement they get from sitting on the ball to be able to focus and do homework, they will never get the work done no matter how much they want the reward. Their nervous system needs the input to perform. This is why rewards don't always work.

> Fuel can't be the reward if it's vital for the engine to run.
>
> It's like turning the key in your car and not understanding why it won't run when there is no gas.

These are usually the kids who have lost recess because of their behavior or lack of production. Now they sit. Sometimes they sit in the principal's office waiting to go back to class after they've, "learned their lesson" only to do it all over again because they haven't gotten what they need to allow them to be successful.

We must remember... *IF THEY COULD, THEY WOULD.*

If they don't have the right kind of input to make an impression in the nervous system, there will be no signals to let the brain work. There will be no regulation, no behavior management, no work production, and likely, no self-esteem. We are trying to improve self-esteem, productivity, successful interactions, and feelings of trust and confidence. When we use the same consequences over and over with no change in behavior, we have to begin looking at a different solution to the problem.

GENERAL TOOLBOX IDEAS

- <u>Replace behaviors</u>. When we see behaviors that are inappropriate or potentially a safety risk, we have to remember that the behavior we are observing serves a purpose. Instead of asking them to stop, try to figure out why they are doing it, and find a more appropriate strategy for them to try. Kids often need assistance for socially appropriate options, and this assistance should be one on one and in a situation that doesn't get interrupted by the dragon.
- <u>Deep Pressure.</u>
- -Bear hugs: face child away from you if you are in a school setting or they don't like the face-to-face contact.
- -Self-hugs: little kids who miss parents while at school can squeeze hard for a self-hug and blow a kiss to mom or dad that will stick until they can do it for real at home.
- -Try games of taco, burrito, hamburger, where cushions are the buns/tortilla and condiments can be put on top. Pressing into the cushions will give slow, deep organizing pressure.
- <u>Try to catch kids being good</u>. Even a wink or verbal praise can do the trick. Be specific about the praise so they know what they are doing right.
- <u>Allow *time* to reset and recover.</u> When the nervous system goes into fight or flight, it doesn't often bounce back easily or quickly. Allowing for time and even a different setting can help with this transition back to a regulated state. Many kids need 5-7 seconds to process what we are saying; this is a long time! Behavior can appear defiant if we don't wait long enough.
- <u>Respect preferences.</u> Many kids will show us exactly what they can handle through their behavior. Forcing a "get used to it" approach sets off the nervous system and takes them away from the logical part of their world and into dragon territory.

- <u>Take a moment and breathe</u>. Just slowing the world down for a moment, with some deep breathing and mindfulness, can go a long way in recovery and regulation. Have your child close their eyes and focus on what they can hear, smell, taste, and how they are breathing.
- <u>Create a Picture Schedule.</u> Use a picture to prepare kids for what is coming. Images are fast to process and don't leave anything unknown because it is right in front of them. You can show them the sequence of an activity, what the day looks like or what the finished product should be.

SENSORY PROCESSING SIGNALS

The brain and body must always be communicating. Our brain needs information from the body to analyze what's been felt, smelled, tasted, etc. Our body needs information from the brain to know how and when to respond. Behavior is a response. It is a communication method, and signals are a *huge* part of communication.

Our brain must be able to process all the sensory information in our body and from our world, or we won't be able to survive. This is *sensory processing*. Another way to think of this is similar to a bunch of wires with connectors. Input, coming in from the world or our body, goes up this wire and creates a signal to be analyzed. Signals tell us that information has come in and is available for the brain to read and instruct the body what to do. Different kinds of sensations create effective communication which is why play and using all the senses is so important.

Sensory integration is when the system or thinking brain receives this input, organizes it, and knows how to make a response based on how the other systems are working. Now this information can be sent back down to the body, and we get a quick and appropriate response. It can also be generalized and applied to different situations with little difficulty. Behavior is dependent upon how the brain integrates information to make a response.

Every system is different. Things that might completely repulse one person may not even be noticed by someone else. Previous experiences will affect how you feel about the input coming into your system which is then stored for later use. When your system can quickly analyze if something is good, then you are more available for learning. When your system recognizes something as bad or dangerous, it quickly responds with a fight, flight, or freeze reaction to protect. When you pull your hand away from something hot before getting burned, your nervous system and brain are responding from experience. All of this is critical for survival.

It's painful to watch your child as they continue to miss the cues that help them navigate their world. When success is hard to find and friends are nowhere to be found, our kids begin to give up because nothing ever works out for them.

THE DRAGON PHENOMENON

The dragon phenomenon was created to provide a different way to talk about signals with kids. My son loved dragons, and dragons have fire... this is how they communicate. If you see flames everywhere, you know to watch out! Pretty effective communication if you ask me! Many things happen along this road of life that make playing school or getting along with others very difficult. Sometimes it is the way our child is wired that makes these skills hard to come by. Sometimes these skills are slow to develop, or sometimes the signals that are meant to warn us don't work. If we can assume that poor behavior is related to signal issues, maybe it will help us see our child through a different lens.

We need to be able to monitor these signals because if something is off, the signals will alert the brain, and it can adjust. This is where the dragon becomes a handy tool. Imagine a dragon who lives in the limbic system or center of our brain. I call this area the dragon cave. This cave sits at the base of all our thinking power. It is where the signals come from and how the thinking brain feels what is going on. It is easy to see that even a smart thinking brain can't work if the signals coming from the cave are off. Signals and skills are both needed. The cave is where the feelings come together to create signals that instruct the thinking brain.

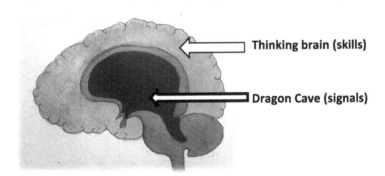

The dragon who lives in this cave is critical because we count on warnings to keep our thinking brain informed to stay safe and be able to regulate. We need the right amount of signals for our brain to work... too many or too few mean trouble!

- Sometimes there is a fire dragon in the cave who sends out too many signals all the time!
- Other times we are dealing with a sleeping dragon who is completely clueless and not giving any signals at all... even when we need them!

When the dragon is in check, the child can work their magic. They can laugh with friends, listen, and figure out what they need to do. When this kind of self-regulation happens, they have the magic to calm or wake the dragon, and they also know how to use him to make life safe and easy. We need to be able to handle dragon problems so we can be safe, logical, successful... *and regulated*.

Dragon power can get out of balance and what happens then is likely what you are experiencing now... *yuck*! While it might take time for the dragon to evolve or to calm down, just being aware of how this character works in your child's system will help you move toward finding balance with the signals.

First you need to identify if you are dealing with too many signals, such as with a fire dragon, or not enough signals like with a sleepy dragon, in *this* moment. Be aware that you will often deal with both these pesky guys, but usually one more than the other. Our wiring seems to determine which dragon shows up more, but there are situations where a new issue or dragon may show up out of nowhere. Are too many alarms going off, or is the dragon out to lunch? These dragons can be tamed, and they will evolve... I promise!

SLEEPY DRAGONS

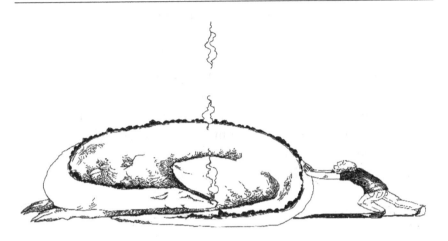

Sleepy dragons are tricky because you will think all is well until it suddenly isn't! If your child has too much sleepy dragon they can usually handle new people, new activities, and any change is often easy for them because they don't have signals flying everywhere telling them to be aware. Not all sleepy dragons cause kids to seek out crazy, dangerous activities, and sometimes the lack of signals may only affect them in specific areas of life that are not as obvious or as scary as others.

School can be tough with sleepy dragons in charge because kids don't get the signal to listen, so they miss instruction, and now they don't know when or how to start working. Success can be hard to find, no matter how smart they are. Warnings need to help kids attend to the homework assignment or work project that should be started *now* instead of Thursday night when it is due Friday. This feeling of heat and uneasiness can be useful because this dragon's job is to alert them, and what better way to get their attention than through fire and rumbling?

The Sleepy Dragon was the first dragon I created because of my son. He seemed to constantly miss cues in his environment, especially at school but also socially. These kids can be tough to parent because they really believe they know the how and when. Even with no experience, he thought he had it all figured out. There was no convincing him otherwise and often he had to live through the crash before his dragon would even stir. And then, even after a major upset, he seemed to forget almost instantly what had just happened, only to repeat these behaviors again and again. I was watching from the sidelines and could do nothing to help... I needed his dragon's attention!

FIRE DRAGONS

When there are too many signals and our dragon is always shooting flames, it does *not* feel good! This feeling inside can keep us from trying new things, interacting with new people, and essentially keep us from anything new. Anxiety is a very common issue with people who have too many signals, and these constant worries can be exhausting… for everyone involved!

One of the good things about this fire dragon issue is that you probably do not need to constantly remind your child to wear a helmet when riding their bike or stressing over how high they may be climbing in the neighbor's tree. Nope, they are not a problem in this way, ever! They are usually good at doing homework well before it is due because of all the "what if" signals that make their tummy hurt if they aren't organized and on top of everything.

Behavior issues often stem from anxiety. Aggressive and loud behavior can come from too many signals and way too much fire. The class bully is often a kiddo who is insecure and afraid, so they act to counteract how they are feeling inside. When the brain switches into protection mode, more and more stress hormones are released. This vicious cycle can create behaviors that are erratic and often misunderstood. Disorders such as anxiety, obsessive-compulsive tendencies, and even attentional deficits can be diagnosed when really the brain is just struggling to deal with all the incoming information.

Things to consider with fire dragons:

- If kids can't weed out all the incoming signals, they will seem distracted and have lots of "squirrel moments" that are unfocused and distracted. (My wiring causes me to get distracted by the simplest of things, and even the best-trained dogs react when they see a squirrel, thus the saying "squirrel moments.")
- If kids are not sure how something is going to feel at any moment, they will try to control it through behavior, and that might appear obsessive-compulsive, aggressive, or like they are avoiding things.
- If everything makes fire, you can be left with a kid who overreacts and seems emotionally fragile.
- Sometimes the well-meaning strategy of prepping kids for what is to come turns into a complete worry fest, and now they hyper-focus on the scary stuff all week. You will figure this out real fast with your child, so just being aware of this in their wiring will help you adjust next time.

This dragon was a key player in my daughter's wiring. I had learned through dealing with her older brother that preparation made life easier. Now however, I was dealing with worries and anxiety from the moment I began prepping her for the doctor appointment coming on Thursday. She was completely consumed with fear for four days, and the drive to that appointment was borderline impossible. "What if I get a shot?" was the question of the week… every hour, every day, and always dramatic.

No explanation would help. I eventually stopped prepping her and waited for the response when she realized we were parking at the doctor's office. I figured I could sweep her into the waiting room and at least the meltdown would only be as long as the appointment would take. Eventually, as she got older with more experience, the preparation and advance notice was, and still is, helpful, but when she was little, I had to completely re-think my approach.

The result of too much fire dragon is exhausting, for everyone!

THE NUMBER ONE REASON WE TALK ABOUT DRAGONS IS TO PRESERVE SELF ESTEEM!

The dragon allows for a judgment-free way to discuss how your child is behaving in that moment. It can help your child understand how the signals work in their brain. They might even figure out that they have some control over this relatively temporary issue that is making them feel awful! Now they can help come up with strategies to tame a fire dragon or wake up the completely useless sleeping dragon. When you can see your child's flaws as a dragon issue, there is something to solve, not something wrong with your child. They just have a dragon issue to deal with, and the goal is to find balance.

Children who struggle with the sleepy dragon are often asked:

- "Why didn't you get that done?"
- "Why are we in the emergency room again?"
- "Why didn't you hand in your homework?"

Children who struggle with those fire dragons are often asked:

- "Why are you scared of that?"
- "Why won't you go to that birthday party?"
- "Why are you crying? There's nothing to cry about."

The cool thing about the pesky dragon is that he can help us talk about tough behavior, and it even gives us fun ways to explain the yucky feelings we sometimes get. After all, isn't it that crazy dragon that needs to relax or wake up? Now we have something to focus on, a non-threatening way to find balance instead of another opportunity to point out why our child is failing us. Blowing out flames or helping manage the fire dragon is now something quite manageable, and a great way to discuss things related to how a child is feeling inside.

IF WE CAN TEACH OUR CHILDREN THAT PEOPLE, ALL PEOPLE, DEAL WITH DRAGON OR SIGNAL ISSUES, IT MIGHT HELP THEM TO REMEMBER THAT THE PERSON IS STILL VALUABLE AND WORTH KNOWING. THIS PERSON MIGHT BE WORKING THROUGH SOMETHING THAT IS AFFECTING HOW THEY APPEAR OR BEHAVE.

Don't get me wrong. I too value the importance of self-responsibility. Is it okay to blame something else when your child is misbehaving? Raising children to be thoughtful, insightful, and happy people requires self-reflection, which means we must take responsibility for our actions. If we find someone or something to blame, we may never see our role in this process to change it. The concept here is simply an introduction to baby steps that will eventually allow your child to see what is going on. When kids are continually failing, their nervous system is so shut down that they are often incapable of taking responsibility and turning it into something positive for future learning to occur.

Our family discussions now covered the fact that my daughter experienced a lot more fire dragon, and her brother usually had a completely useless, sleepy dragon. It was fun to talk about dragons. She began to understand why he did things that drove her positively crazy! He does get some signals, so at least he doesn't bounce off a cliff, but those little things that can be a big deal in the real world just weren't getting enough attention. Homework and those projects that needed to be turned in didn't worry him enough. His specific wiring made him more prone to the sleepy dragon, so he waited until the last second until it was physically impossible to complete the work, and the meltdown ensued.

There are certainly times when my son deals with a fire dragon, and my daughter's dragon is completely useless. But overall, they are pretty consistent. When we have balance where we need it, we can feel good, pay attention, and be able to take in our world. We are *regulated*. It really doesn't matter which dragon your child is more prone to as long as they can figure out what is going on inside so they can counteract those feelings with strategies.

Through the course of dragon talk with my children, I realized that my own dragon holds me back too, even as an adult. Have you ever created patterns or habits but not really been able to explain why? Some people hate parades, or museums. I found that I would avoid even going to a grocery store on the weekend. Sounds kind of silly or inconsequential, but I would rather run out of basic supplies than go shopping on Saturday when everyone else is there. I love my quiet Monday shopping schedule. I don't like crowds, I don't like shopping, and I definitely don't want the two at one time... way too many alarms going off!

Many times we can identify traits in our own wiring only to discover that our child may be dealing with the same issue, but with more intensity. When I was explaining to my daughter about the dragon, she realized that my fear of crowds and shopping was probably a dragon issue that totally explained why I didn't go to the store on the weekend. My dragon was being silly! I had no idea if it would be crowded at the store, but the alarms prevented me from even checking it out. While this scenario really isn't an issue that affects my ability to successfully function in life, it is still pretty irritating when we run out of milk!

Some kids don't like dragons, or maybe dragons aren't a useful tool for their communication. There are many other ways to chat about how they feel or how they are behaving. The key here is to find something, anything, that is fun to use when solving problems related to signals. This will depend on who your kid is, what their interests are, and where they are developmentally.

- A young child might love Disney characters, animals, or princesses. Let them figure out what they relate to if they don't like the dragon. The concept and problem-solving will be the same but the character they use might affect their motivation and buy-in for finding a solution.
- Children with special needs may be older but at a different level developmentally than their peers. If they come up with the character, it will be more powerful for them, and their imagination will take over. Don't worry about age-appropriate characters... focus on relatability.
- Some kids respond more to the computer analogy. Computer systems can lag and prevent us from getting the information we need, just like the sleeping dragon. They can glitch or overheat when there is too much going on, or they have been on too long, just like the fire dragon.
- There are also many commercial items such as The Alert Program (or How is Your Engine Running) by Williams & Shellenberger, Tool Chest by Diana Henry, and The Zones of Regulation by Leah Kuypers. These are a few fantastic resources that are already out there and ready to use.

If your child has an area of interest, see if they can come up with a way to use their interest as a tool for communication. It will be motivating because they came up with it, and it will help them relate to their body and emotions in a way that fits their developmental and cognitive level.

THE GOAL ISN'T DRAGONS.

THE GOAL IS UNDERSTANDING SIGNALS AND FIGURING OUT HOW TO FEEL BETTER.

MANAGING SIGNALS

Self-monitoring is required if strategies are going to help you manage signals because the use of strategies depends on the ability to know what is going on inside and outside. Is there a buzz in the lights? Is someone tapping a pencil? Is the tag in the shirt rubbing too hard? Is the smell of perfume distracting? Is the room too hot, too dark, too loud?

Sometimes dragons need to let your child do a quick body scan. Am I hungry? Do I need to use the bathroom? Am I thirsty? Sometimes things that should be automatic just aren't, and realizing them through this scan can significantly affect behavior. The scan will help you figure out what strategies to try.

Our sensory system is designed to give us helpful information about our body and our world so we can stay safe and *regulated*. There are times when the dragon can take it all in and helpfully manage things. When the dragon can't, we must help him out. We need to do some dragon taming!

The best place to start coming up with ideas for strategies is with the three primary roots that most significantly impact our sensory system. Roots are where all the stability comes from, so it makes sense that this is where to focus. You can come up with many strategies on your own just by remembering what these foundational roots are.

vestibular   tactile

proprioception

**<u>IF THE ROOTS AREN'T
SOLID, NEITHER
IS THE TREE.</u>**

The three primary roots that affect everything are tactile, vestibular, and proprioception.

See if you can figure out which one your child can use right now.

1. <u>Proprioception</u>: This involves sensors in our joints and muscles to tell us where our body is and how much force we need to use, all of which helps us control our body movements. Proprioception is usually a good place to start because any activity that involves using muscles and heavy force will be easier for the system to organize and process. Strategies here might include chores, games, or even fun weight-lifting activities. You can make up jobs like carrying books from one corner of the room to another. You may not care where a heavy pile of books ends up, but after they are moved you may be dealing with a very different dragon!

2. <u>Tactile</u>: This involves anything we touch which helps the rest of the system regulate. Being able to tolerate and soothe with touch is very important. Think about your child when they were upset as a baby. Did they play with the tag on their blanket, your hair as you held them, or your jewelry? Strategies might include providing fidget tools or something with texture. Knowing what touch they don't like is equally notable. If the feeling of a tag is scratchy and sets off too many signals, nothing else can be addressed because this is too distracting or uncomfortable to ignore.

3. <u>Vestibular</u>: This is the input we get from our body and the inner ear that tells us we are tipping, moving, and ultimately out of neutral. We need to be able to tolerate movement and changes in movement to make sense of where our body is in space and

essentially stay safe. Vestibular movement such as swinging is significant input that can wake up sleepy dragons. It is also the one that might be tougher to tolerate especially for those kids who are more sensitive. Strategies here might be rocking back and forth for the calming input and jumping or swinging for more alerting input.

These three roots can be useful for *all* kinds of dragons. Still, not all kids can tolerate all three because there may be developmental holes that affect one or more of these roots. When this happens, the system has trouble recognizing what is going on so it tends to go into protection mode.

If your child is afraid of anything or avoids certain sensory root activities, these preferences and fears *must* be respected. This is not the root to start with when coming up with strategies. Kids avoid or respond for a reason.

We are dealing with *their* dragon, so *they* must be the expert. We don't need more fire right now, we need balance.

STRATEGIES FOR CONTROLLING SIGNALS

Now that you know the importance of signals and how they impact behavior and regulation, it is time to explore the specific strategies. Balance can be hard to find so we need something that makes an impact. Talk of strategies can be fun, and referencing tools in a super cool toolbox is a powerful and effective image. The more tools we have, the more things we can handle. We need tools that help us when the signals aren't working and also for the times when signals are completely overwhelming.

When figuring out what tools to use, you have to consider all the senses. Keep in mind that tools are just that; they aren't the be-all or end-all, and they certainly aren't a magic pill that cures all. Some work, some don't. Some may terrify your child. Some will be just plain fun. The important thing to remember is that if they aren't working, they aren't tools. If your child doesn't want to try one, don't push it. If your child isn't benefitting from one, don't use it. If you see they are misusing it, it's a toy and not a tool so it's time to try something else. It is important that kids know they are the experts but that sometimes they might need a guide. Dragons can be tricky, and we all need help sometimes.

It's important to talk about which type of dragon is hanging out today. You can have a different dragon from day to day, or situation to situation. Kids must recognize what kind of dragon they are training in that moment. If you are dealing with a fire dragon that is trying to get your attention, the strategies will look different than those you might use with a sleepy dragon. We may need to alter the intensity depending on whether we need to wake up the dragon or simply calm him. Sometimes the same movement can be done quickly to wake up a sleepy dragon, or very slowly to calm a fire dragon.

Not every strategy will work for everyone. This is when the detective comes in and your help and observations can be a huge asset. They may be doing the same thing over and over but *you* can learn from their experience because you will remember how they responded last time. You can also coach them to use tools *before* they meltdown. Try as many of the strategies as you can. When your child gets good at monitoring how they feel after using a tool, they might begin coming up with their own ideas. Write them down, draw pictures, and identify which dragon responds to which tool. If they work now, celebrate because this may change tomorrow. But help them begin the process and life-skill of tapping into their dragons and learning to tame them.

USING THE DETECTIVE TO FIGURE OUT THE SIGNALS

The detective will start as a parent, teacher, or anyone in a child's life who can observe behavior and help tame those signals. The ultimate goal is to eventually pass the role of detective to the child so they can figure out *if* they need help, *what* they need, *how* to advocate for this need, and *when* to utilize their tools or strategies. It's a process and the more modeling and consistency, the better the results; independence and success will come faster. The two primary objectives for the detective are the *when* and *what*.

-When do they seem to need input or help? When do you see them trying to use a tool?

-What do they seem to be drawn to or avoid? Is it movement-related? Is it visual or auditory? Is it heavy work?

Points to Consider

- Teach children *how* to use their sensory system to get the kind of input they need. This will empower them to be independent and confident for higher levels of learning.
- When they get the sensory experience their nervous system is craving, they will be able to attend, perform tasks, interact with others appropriately, and demonstrate self-control.
- Appropriate sensory input improves processing and sensory integration and has a lasting effect throughout the day!

USING THE SENSES TO COME UP WITH STRATEGIES

There are many fun ways to distract the system into a calmer or more alert state using our different senses. Think of all the sensory input that comes in when you take a break and walk outside. The light is a different color and intensity; you can feel the wind on your face, smell the air, hear the birds, and even feel the squish beneath your shoes. Make sure to utilize all these senses when coming up with the toolbox.

- What can be done to get more signals going?
- How can unnecessary signals be reduced to avoid fight or flight?

Think of all the different senses we use every day… this is where a lot of knowledge will lie. Even watching what your child is drawn to or avoids will give you a lot of information about their needs. The following are ideas that involve each sensory system, but you and your child will likely come up with many more on your own. If you find some especially helpful areas, make a list of these tools to hang up in plain sight so you will remember to use them.

Touch: Sometimes we can provide tools to feed the tactile system. Don't forget that touch in the mouth is a very powerful tool. Do they put things in their mouth? What do they touch a lot? Do they fiddle with buttons or twirl their hair? Do they fidget during study time or while listening? Remember that what works for some kids, may not work for others. You may not want to use some tools based on what you have observed them avoiding in everyday life.

- Fidget tools during listening time can work great, especially if they offer resistance like hand strengtheners. Even a paper clip and rubber band can make a fidget tool. Remember we don't want these tools to become toys or a weapon.

- Attach different textures like Velcro or texture strips under their desk. The nice thing about this is they can't throw them.
- Provide different textures that can be held in the lap like fleece, fur, slime.
- Have them try sitting in a large, textured bean bag or on a textured carpet square.
- Supply things to suck on like a water bottle or hard candy. Have them chew things like gum or a chewy snack like a bagel.

Vision: Change the environment. What they look at affects how the signals communicate to the brain. Do they prefer to look at bright lights, colorful pictures, bare walls? Pay attention to what they seem to gravitate toward or avoid, and notice their response. Are they over-stimulated with too much visual input? Do they seek empty corners or wear a hoodie sweatshirt all the time? ***

- Increase signals. Provide a bright light or lots of colors and visual detail. Highlight with colorful pens so they notice different details within the text.
- Decrease signals. Use dim lights or filter the light with colored, magnetic fabric over the fluorescent lights in one corner of the room. Irlen filters or colored overlays can affect how visual information is hitting the brain.
- Make a clear workspace. Clutter can be very distracting, and it is the perfect opportunity for "squirrel moments".
- Cover a portion of the page they're working on to prevent their being overwhelmed. Chunking is also a great way to help kids with breaking up material into manageable pieces. Have them only do the part that is showing, then take a break or provide a reward. The content can get longer and longer, but it helps them simply *begin*.
- Use sunglasses or provide an environment with limited visual input. Kids might subtly create this environment using long hair to cover their face or eyes. Hoodies create a safe space that buffers

much of the input that is overwhelming. The fabric dampens noise and prevents peripheral vision. Sometimes what a child chooses to wear or use will tell you a lot about what they need or *don't* need.

***Before demanding that the hood comes off, see if there might be a reason behind the hood. Maybe there are times they can use it, and other times they can take it off. If they can listen and learn when the hood is on, does it matter? What is the goal? If it is learning or participation, maybe that hood is sheer brilliance and one of the tools this child has figured out that helps. This is just something to consider. I know that some kids might appear to want things like a hoodie because they want to do everything you don't want them to do. Helping them see why the hoodie feels good can empower them as experts of their dragon. But remember, there are times we want to have the hood off so our dragon can relax or let them see the real world. They need to get used to hanging out without freaking out.

Hearing: Noise is often a distraction or it creates way too much input. Is your child affected by noise or talking, or are there sounds that irritate or startle them excessively? The school bell, lights buzzing, or a toilet flushing can all mean danger. They sell inexpensive, noise-canceling headphones that work even if you don't want to play music, but having the option for either is nice for most kids.

- Classical music with an even, slow beat can help organize and calm those fire dragons.
- Electronic music created from a computer, or hard rock with uneven beat and loud bass works for the sleepy dragons who can't focus.
- White noise or noisemakers can drown out distractions.
- Hoodie sweatshirts buffer input. I must mention this again because kids love those hoods.
- Noise-cancelling headphones dampen sound.

Smell: While we often forget the power of smell, it is one of the most effective ways to alter regulation. Essential oils and diffusers can be found just about everywhere, and this can completely transform how a space will feel. Incense can be too intense for many children, but if you have one that struggles with too few signals, it's worth a try.

- Calming smells: lavender, valerian, jasmine, vanilla
- Alerting smells: lemon or citrus, peppermint, rosemary, eucalyptus

Taste or Oral Input: Taste can also alter our mood, much like smell. Oral input is a way of describing anything we put in our mouth. Babies come into the world using the power of oral input for soothing, calming and alerting. Those thumbs are useful for many things! Oral input by itself can provide input but introducing various flavors can also affect regulation.

- Alerting flavors can be sour, spicy, minty.
- Oral input can be crunchy food such as popcorn, pretzels, or apples. Chewy food like gum, or bagels work and sour food such as pickles or lemon.
- Heavy work for the mouth can be accomplished using a straw for applesauce, yogurt, or other thick food because it gives powerful input into the mouth.

Movement/Vestibular: This is one of those critical, organizing root senses. But there are specific activities that can be more calming, and then others that are more alerting or energizing. Pay attention to what kind of movement your child craves, like bouncing or crashing into objects. Look at what they might avoid such as high places or feet leaving the ground, swinging, car rides, or even running. Next, look at *when* their system needs a little more or less input. For instance, do they need input in the morning versus afternoon, after homework, or right before chores. All of this is critical in figuring out if the dragon is dead asleep or suddenly shooting fire. Sometimes we see problems more at school because the expectations and social environment are very different from the home environment.

- Activities that provide more input and feed the sleepy dragon can include movement, which tips the head and activates the organs that control the vestibular system. Try things such as jumping up to touch the door frame, playing sports, running, somersaults, and sitting on a large therapy ball or dynamic cushion.

- Activities that decrease input or calm the fire dragon focus more on slower, forward and backward movements that don't tip the head and over-activate the vestibular organs. Activities can include swinging slowly, and rocking forward to backward like in a rocking chair.

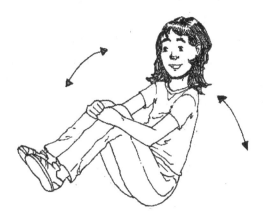

Heavy Work/Proprioception: This is probably the best tool because these activities and strategies can alert *and* calm. When you increase the intensity and difficulty, it is alerting and sends more signals. When you focus on slower, heavier tasks, it is calming and quiets down the signals. Anything that involves working the muscles is organizing for the nervous system.

- Activities that work for any type of regulation issue can include resistive tubing around the legs of a chair so the child can push or pull against it with their feet. Create jobs or games that involve pushing, pulling, or lifting such as erasing the board, putting chairs on the desk, moving furniture, pushups on the floor for sleepy dragons, maybe against the wall for fire dragons, sports, or exercise programs.
- Sensory Diet is a term coined by Patricia Wilbarger, and it refers to any kind of movement or input that can be integrated into someone's day or routine. Much like how we might incorporate

food into our daily schedule, movement-based strategies between and before activities improve regulation, and result in focused attention. You and your child can come up with any kind of movement as long as you are mindful of a few things.

1. Make sure it is easy to implement into their day. School activities need to be subtler so they don't distract the class.
2. Be aware of how your child responds. If it gives them more energy and they can't calm down to *work,* you may need a slower, heavier activity.
3. You can prep their system with heavy, hard work in the morning, and it can stay in their nervous system and improve regulation for 4-6 hours *afterward*. This can start their day out with more success and increase their feeling of competency and independence.

WHEN YOU AREN'T SURE OF THE SIGNALS: STRATEGIES THAT WORK FOR ALL KINDS OF ISSUES

Whether you are dealing with too many or not enough signals, the strategies can be very similar, but small changes can completely alter the effect. If there are no signals, try to increase the speed or intensity to create more signals or wake up the sleeping dragon. If there are too many signals, slow things down or make things heavy to calm down the fire dragon.

Most strategies will work for both dragons, but when kids are in the fight or flight state, they need specific techniques that will put out the fire and control the many signals flying everywhere. If you are unsure which strategies to use and behavior is extreme, start with the specific tools for too many signals or fire dragons, because none of those will over-stimulate the nervous system. These strategies will work on either dragon, so give them a try and see if you can figure out what works.

The goal of strategies is to help the brain process information. If we can process, we can manage our behavior, determine what we might need, and regulate. But nothing can happen if the brain isn't able to process.

> The brain cannot process *and* protect at the same time.
>
> The brain cannot process if it isn't getting signals.

SIGNAL STRATEGIES

-Carry heavy Objects

-Deep Breaths

-Give a hug

-Chair pushup

-Push hands Together-hard

Helper Squishes

-Rocking

-Find a Quiet Space

- <u>Dynamic sitting options:</u> Cushions, big therapy balls, and standing are great ways to help kids get the input they need to wake up their sleepy dragon. When we have to put effort into our postural muscles, it keeps us alert. The cushions give a feeling similar to a big ball without the trouble of transporting it around, and  work well for kids who might not be coordinated enough to sit on a ball safely.

- <u>Eat or drink something:</u> Chewy stuff like bagels or gum gives strong input into the jaw muscles and helps regulate the nervous system. Sips of water, especially cold, can also create enough input to begin affecting focused attention. *Getting up* to get the drink gives even more input. Gum and chewing on something while working can help to focus attention. Chewable items or jewelry  are often used with autism, very young children or kids with sensory processing issues.

- <u>Movement:</u> Remember, every time we move our bodies, we get a good shot of endorphins that help wake us up. This can happen in the morning as a "dragon workout" because it can last for hours in the nervous system. Studies  indicate significant benefit of movement, even 20-40 minutes three times per week can positively affect the mind and body.

- <u>Motivators:</u> Providing quick breaks or rewards after chunks of work are complete can provide the motivation to push through stuff they don't like and improve their feelings of independence and success.

- <u>Extension of the body:</u> When we lie on our stomach, we get extension of the neck which is alerting and will create more signals.

- <u>Sometimes we need to add external reminders or alarms</u>. These can be reminders on smartphones, checklists in obvious places or even a schedule or list written on the bathroom mirror with a dry erase marker. Helping kids with the details of their world can lead to improved habits that prevent dragons from getting in the way of success.

- <u>Chunking:</u> Whenever you can break up work or projects, it helps make the task more manageable and less overwhelming.

DRAGON TAMING TO ADJUST THE SIGNALS

Talking about dragons with kids is fun! They come up with all kinds of dragons, and even ways those dragons can be real stinkers. Discussing ways to tame a dragon encourages kids to self-monitor and begin the process of self-regulation, which we know is critical for happiness in life.

Don't forget that it is almost impossible to come up with self-monitoring strategies in the moment or at times of fight or flight. Figuring out how to monitor signals should happen when no one is upset or they won't work. The same goes for dragon taming. Dragon talk allows the child to think out of the box at a time when things can be fun and their nervous system isn't trying to protect them. They aren't in trouble and they haven't screwed up again. Their dragon may have some issues, but your child is still in the driver's seat, and their brain will work for them as long as they don't feel threatened. *We don't want to problem-solve or strategize when the system is in protection mode!*

Kids can come up with ideas or try out your ideas. For times when the dragon takes over and their brain doesn't work, they can refer to posters they make to show them strategies that help them feel better. Get creative! The goal is to empower kids to make good choices. When they are demonstrating successful and positive behavior, the dragon balance is working, which means they are Master Dragon Tamers! How's that for a title?

AWARD OF EXCELLENCE

DRAGON TAMING

AWARDED TO:

_____

FOR MASTERY IN THE ART
OF DRAGON TAMING

FIGHT, FLIGHT, OR FREEZE

HOW IT AFFECTS SIGNALS AND REGULATION

When our system gets bombarded with too much input, like when signals go astray, it can quickly put us into what's called fight, flight, or freeze. It is our most primitive system, and we tend to fall back on it when we are stressed. We don't have to be going through an actual life or death experience because the *perception* of danger can be enough to trigger this response. Even though our child isn't in real danger, their system may be perceiving excessive stress and falling into this protection mode.

Fight can look like just that, and freeze is that state of shut down where you just don't get a reaction. Flight can be a little trickier. It can be avoidance, excuses, daydreaming, or blaming. Much of this is subconscious, and your child may not even realize what is going on. It all ends the same way: difficulty navigating social situations, trouble listening, focusing, learning, or behaving. Essentially the nervous system is preparing to protect. This is usually in the form of fighting or running, so the blood flow is preserved for the limbs and no longer going to the thinking brain. Protection and processing can't happen at the same time, so math and navigating a scary social situation at school won't work if the brain isn't working!

Imagine you are walking alone in a dark parking lot and you realize you are being followed. You might not notice you stubbed your toe, and you certainly can't remember what is on your grocery list right now! You are afraid, and your senses are tuned into safety. This is a fight or flight response that is appropriate. When your child experiences this same physiological reaction every day with every activity they are doing, we begin to see that life can get pretty exhausting.

When a child is in fight, flight, or freeze mode, we need to understand the emotional reaction. Even with our encouragement and even if it seems like no big deal to us, this mechanism prevents them from being logical. Something like recess, which is anticipated with glee by many, can be the biggest hurdle of the day for the child who doesn't know *how* that unstructured time will feel. Things that seem completely harmless, like showing the class your most loved toy for show-and-tell, can feel like our parking lot example above. *We need protection*! Even the most well-meaning parents can put their child into fight or flight by demanding they go and experience a friend's birthday party. Birthday parties are always fun, right?

Some think if we simply raise the expectations, kids will try harder and see that everything is really fun and ok. The only problem here is that they already can't do what we're asking, so raising expectations isn't the answer either. We could tell them a story about when we were little and how fun it was to go to the water park, and it was a big one, nothing like the one we are looking at right now. Sadly, processing this story doesn't work when there are already too many signals. It doesn't matter that all their friends are right there telling them how much fun they are about to have. *Nothing* matters except being safe. That's what the dragon is saying, so it must be true!

> A child might just react and not even realize how they
> are behaving. Dragons are good at masking a situation
> and they make it really hard for a child to make a
> good, logical choice or to regulate their behavior.

ALL children want to be successful, but some can't, no matter how hard they try.

The perception and *emotion* of what's coming in is very real. Therefore, we often see poor behavior at unexpected times. If something comes in and it is perceived as scary, the resulting behavior will reflect this emotion. Worse yet, this child might not even know they are misbehaving. This behavior can be referred to as drama or over-reaction. At the end of the day, it is very real for this child, and the "deal with it" approach probably won't help them wrap their brain around it.

STRATEGIES FOR FIGHT, FLIGHT, OR FREEZE

Right now it doesn't matter why the dragon is freaking out. The goal is to help your child find balance so they have a fair chance of determining if this will actually be fun. This is where all your previous dragon talk will come in handy. If they already know that they are wired a little more on the sensitive side and that their threshold is usually pretty low, you might be able to convince them that it's just the dragon over-responding. We don't want them to feel defensive and attacked because then they won't be able to adapt. Maybe they can manage this situation after all. They may need your help, but pushing faster, louder, and harder will only increase the protective response we are trying to prevent.

So where do we even start? First, we know what our child's wiring sets them up for. A sleepy dragon is very different than a fire dragon, and that is the first thing to acknowledge. Your mellow child may be showing fire dragon behaviors, so trying to figure out the trigger is a good place to start. Is this behavior typical in instances like this, or is there something new that may have caused a problem? Identifying what came right before the behavior can often give you insight and lead you to a solution.

Many times, simply providing for *anticipation* will help the thinking brain overpower the silly dragon signals. If I know that something is happening later in my day that is tough or stressful, I can work on backup plans to get me through. I can begin to form a picture in my head about what it might feel like and then how to manage those feelings. I can get my system ready and bypass protection mode.

Pictures, planners, calendars, and lists are great ways to help anyone anticipate what is coming. They allow for processing before the protection phase. Don't think your child is too smart, too young, or doesn't care. It is surprising how helpful it is to know what the day looks like, or what an activity looks like step-by-step. This can often be enough to prevent problems, even for kiddos that don't experience that fire dragon very often. Again, this depends on your child's wiring and your memory of how they respond. If anticipation sets them off right away and they are unable to create that backup plan because of this stress, they are clearly not ready for this approach.

Remember that even really bright kids might not know how to do something that we might think should be easy. It can be hard to imagine, but some kids don't know *how* to play! Play should come naturally, but there is a lot that goes into this skill. They may do everything to keep you from knowing this, but when they don't know how to play, their behavior will be anything but playful. Sometimes kids will come up with creative ways to disguise that they really have no idea how to participate.

One of my favorite teachers once told me she always tries to get recess duty. This seemed strange to me because recess is a lovely, quiet time for teachers to re-group, plan, and exhale. This amazing teacher quickly figured out that the kids in her class didn't all know what to do at recess and this caused a lot of stress in their day. Sure, you see the kids who go grab a ball or a swing, but there were a lot of them who truly didn't know how to navigate the unstructured time of recess.

She made a point to be out there and show them games, or different ways to ask for a turn. She also loved the time to just be out there; she was available for them. The stories the kids shared with her in this unstructured time also helped her figure out a little more about how they were wired and how to better teach them. As adults, we sometimes forget that simple things like play, can actually be quite a mystery for some kids.

Thank you, Joanna Kaiser!

Avoiding stressful situations, especially for those who *do* experience the fire dragon a lot, can make a big difference. Conquering fear requires experiencing what scares them, but this often needs to happen gradually. We want to expose them *slowly* to the input in the world that creates stress. This can mean showing them pictures first, then videos, then real objects or opportunities as we help them begin to manage what they are afraid of. It is also important to remember that what is fun for a sibling or us may *not* be fun for this child. Try to avoid any movie or video game that gets the heart racing or causes those jump scares. There is already enough stress in their world that they must endure and can't control. They don't need more pathways for protection mode when they have to go to recess. The more that dragon *can* react, the more he *will* react. Preventing this as much as possible is critical because there's nothing worse than a big-headed dragon. If he thinks he rules the roost, he really will!

Sadly, we cannot always have the foresight, communication, and ability to avoid every situation that comes along and puts our child into fight or flight. Recovery is critical. Every poor behavior and every stressful event, provides an opportunity to *recover*. Stuff happens. How they respond to that stuff is what begins to define who our child is. It is what teaches them to endure and trust in themselves. It is important to include this in the conversation with your child. If they can try a strategy and then analyze its effectiveness with you later, you have begun the life-long journey of self-monitoring and regulation. Calming strategies provide ideas that can help the nervous system reset and calm down, so your child can feel some control over those feelings inside.

CALMING STRATEGIES

REMEMBER TO RESPECT YOUR CHILD'S CUES AND PREFERENCES

They can show you very quickly if something isn't helping. What might work for one child may be awful for another.

- Pre-teaching, practicing, and role-playing. It is hard to feel calm and centered when you don't know what is coming or how to do something. Skills are just that; they don't always come naturally. Many fight-or-flight moments can come from the simplest skill deficit or not knowing what is coming next.

- Quiet breaks with dim lighting or even better, complete darkness. The nervous system can reset when the visual system is shut down for a bit. Focus on the different sensations that don't involve vision. What do they hear right now? What can they feel? Can they smell anything? This engages other parts of the brain and serves as a great distraction that can totally confuse a fire dragon and calm him down.

- Anything oral is soothing. Think about how your child soothed as a baby. It probably involved sucking on a pacifier or their thumb. Sucking yogurt or other thick food through a straw can provide the oral soothing, but also involve some heavy work for the mouth; proprioception and heavy work are important for regulation.

- Swinging or rocking in a linear direction. Again, how do we soothe babies? We rock them. This is organizing for the nervous system and allows for the vestibular system to be engaged. Only rock or swing forward and backward, never rotational or in a circle because that can result in an already over-stimulated threshold to be hit more than it already is, which completely defeats our purpose.

- Deep touch, firm massage, or vibrating massagers. Deep touch is very organizing to the nervous system because it involves the tactile system, which is a root for strategies. Deep touch can be very effective. Some kids like light touch and vibration while others absolutely do not, so if something seems to be agitating, stop and try something else.

- Simplify their world. Use very few words, reduce visual clutter, move to a different space, allow time for quiet and time to just *be*. Give them permission to be and focus on *recovery*.
- Listen to quiet music. Stimulating different areas of the brain can distract or calm.

WORRIES

When there are too many signals, we get lots of worries and are often in a fight, flight, or freeze state. This can look like aggression, and we may forget that this can be due to worries. The child who acts so tough may be dealing with daily anxiety. Most children with foundational or sensory processing issues, or those who are simply surviving, have plenty of anxiety. This can be challenging because it can prevent them from experiencing the very thing that will help their system develop and adapt.

If we don't have a clear understanding of our own wiring and what dragon we might be prone to, we may be creating anxiety in our child without even knowing it. Many kids, and frankly many adults too, can be significantly affected by the energy in their world. When kids are stressed and we as parents are stressed too, it is tough to help them find balance.  Keeping your anxiety and worries in check is important so that when you are talking to your child, they aren't feeding off of your nervous energy. Remember too, that no one should have a conversation in the moment of stress because the brain isn't functioning adequately and there is way too much smoke!

If you have more than one child, you probably know that once you figure them out, the next child begins to struggle in a completely different way. Back to the drawing board! I used to laugh when they were little because it was almost like a bad game of whack-a-mole. One problem would finally be resolved only to be replaced with another.

I knew my daughter was completely different than my son, even when I was pregnant. She would roll over gently and gracefully every couple of hours compared to the wrestling match my son was having with my bladder. When she was born, she slept! As she grew, I would marvel at how she would hang back and watch instead of impulsively jumping in without instructions. She is emotional, has trouble with last-minute changes, and doesn't like to be pressured or hurried. She will sit and write for hours and still have the diligence to put a smiley-face emoji at the end of seventeen pages. Her wiring is completely different than what I expected and it never occurred to me that it would so profoundly affect my parenting approach.

This I was *not* used to! I was used to flying by the seat of my pants because that is what my son needed. I had just figured this all out.

Now however, I had a *new* problem!

I embarked on a different adventure to help my daughter manage her worries. Like with my son, I researched, talked to friends, professionals, and tried all the strategies and techniques I could. Knowing that fears are related to her wiring helped me remember that she needed to discuss them. But at times, it seemed like all we did was talk about the same worries, and those were getting bigger! Even though she could recognize how silly they were, they were still very much there.

We began strategizing, and we talked about *her* dragon.

- Is your dragon reasonable right now?
- Are you in actual danger?
- Have you already talked out this worry, but your dragon wasn't paying attention and completely missed it?

Time for a dragon time out! Tweak this depending on the age of your child, but it can be fun… and funny, especially when you get your child involved in the dragon storytelling!

Psychologists and family/child counselors have many more tricks. Getting help early can decrease issues that crop up later in life. I recommend this route if the things you are trying aren't working. Some of the strategies that I have used not only with clients but also with my daughter have really helped, and even some that didn't seem to work at first suddenly made a huge difference as she got older. Never hesitate to try out old, previously attempted strategies.

I will never forget as an early therapist, I went to a conference on autism. The guest speaker spoke to an entire room of therapists, sharing his perspective about life with this disability. As someone who feels different from others every day and therefore very anxious about social anything, he shared ways that he managed his anxiety.

Suddenly, his PowerPoint quit working. This completely derailed him and it was clear that he had no idea how to recover. Luckily in a room full of therapists, there was lots of love and understanding. When he finally did recover, he went into more personal and emotional detail than I had ever heard from a public speaker. This experience he just shared with all of us, and the process of recovery as a group, made him completely vulnerable yet comfortable so now all he could do was talk.

He was off script and it was amazing. He told us that when he was a teenager, he had figured out that life was like a play. If he could rehearse every possible scenario, he was able to cope. I don't even think he was aware of the details until this very moment because he almost looked surprised as he was telling us of his struggle during adolescence.

This PowerPoint situation was not on his radar, he hadn't rehearsed it, and he had no backup plan. Kids are no different! Our first response is often our rehearsed response. Talk to your child about a backup plan for those unexpected situations.

My daughter went to an amazing assembly at her middle school, and she came home with a newfound awareness about social media's impact on teen anxiety, depression, and suicide. This is where I found another great tool that quickly became a strategy in our home.

The goal is to give eight hugs per day, and each hug is eight seconds long.

This sounded easy enough, and even though we aren't a super touchy family, it was fun to do. Sometimes I would grab my baby boy who is now way taller than I am, and not a hugger, and just start counting, slowly, to eight. When I saw worries begin to surface with my daughter, I could swoop in, usually giggling because of how fun this new strategy was, and start counting. Soon the eight seconds didn't feel like the eternity it had at the beginning, and I could see a massive shift in the energy of the house. My daughter's worries began to melt away, and her recovery time was much better. We know how important touch is, and this one was a real keeper!

(The speaker at the assembly was Collin Kartchner, who was a social activist and youth advocate who started a movement to #SAVETHEKIDS.)

STRATEGIES FOR WORRIERS

- Take time to be in the moment with your child to really listen, and remember to give them plenty of time to respond. Even just being together in a quiet room can do more for their worries than you could ever imagine; hugs work too! Eight hugs, eight seconds each.
- Worry rocks can be helpful. You essentially go out and find the perfect stone. It can be smooth, small, a particular shape or color, but you find it together and your child chooses the perfect one for their worries. You can even pick one to use for your worries. This rock can be tucked in a pocket or sit on the nightstand. It can be held, rubbed, put in a special box, or just be there to remind your child that they can handle those worries. You can get creative and make a worry bracelet too.
- One of my favorite books is <u>What to Do When You Worry Too Much</u> by Dawn Huebner. It's written for children and is an excellent tool for them to use because it compares worries to a plant. The more you tend to your plant, the bigger it will get. Worries are the same. The more you focus on your worries throughout the day, the bigger they will get. The author uses an imaginary worry box that you can't open until worry talk time. Over time the worry box isn't as full because many of those worries are soon forgotten when they're not the focus of the day. This is a great book I highly recommend!
- A visual schedule is as simple as it sounds! It doesn't matter if you use pictures in an app, scribbled on a calendar, words on a chart, or dry erase on the bathroom mirror. What is important is that your child has an idea of the schedule and can see what is coming so they can anticipate and better know how to deal with the process and emotions. A feeling of control is critical when managing worries.
- Break up activities that are difficult or lengthy. This can help with anxiety because many times children know when they have missed what was being asked. When kids are unsure about their ability, anxiety results.

- A worry journal is a great way to get the concerns out so you can attempt to let them out of your head. These can be in picture form too, depending on your child's preference.
- Role-play the various situations your child might face. When we are anxious, our system goes into fight or flight mode, and quite literally our brain turns off. No more problem solving. No more social skills. No more emotional stability. The next time your child melts down, see if you can find a reason. Whether the issue is over-stimulation, hunger, fatigue, or not having a backup plan, roleplaying can help prevent these situations or at least provide some tools to use when the unexpected just happens.
- Over-scheduling children can prevent imaginative play by not allowing them to figure out what to do with themselves when they are bored. It's surprising how much anxiety comes from not knowing what to do with your time!
- Take pictures of things that worry them so you can talk about it when they are in thinking mode. The first day of school and doctor appointments worry most people, but if you can walk through what is going to happen in your head and get a picture of it, suddenly you can move on. Worriers have trouble moving on. They continue to go back to those situations and worry.
- Remember that we get the behavior we give attention to. If we pay a lot of attention to our worries, they will always be present. If we can shift our focus to something positive, the thoughts that seem to stick are positive. Have your child think of three things that were good about their day, and then one thing they want to focus on for tomorrow to make someone else's day better. If your child doesn't like to write or isn't the journaling type, maybe this makes for good dinner conversation. Try to make this a regular part of their world; try to do it every single day. When you do it out loud and share ideas as a family, it also helps those who might struggle with coming up with ways to see the good, or ways to make people happy.

A child new to middle school experienced true panic at the thought of changing classes. One class was okay but more created way too many opportunities for the unknown. We decided to walk through the hall after school and take pictures of each of her classes. We printed the pictures and put them in order on her schedule. We were able to talk about the process of change and her mom even used this same approach to prep her from home. This conversation with the visuals is a very powerful tool to help expose the nervous system to input, but in a less intense way. She needed to remember to spend less time on the worries, but acknowledging and planning for the unknown allowed her to come up with ideas she could use when she was in the moment. When she was able to see the potential problem, she could process it and *move on*.

THRESHOLDS

HOW THEY AFFECT REGULATION AND SIGNALS

We all have a threshold for input, and it is largely dependent on wiring. A threshold is the point where we can make a response to everything in our world and it is directly related to signals. We need to hit this threshold to engage, attend, and focus, but we also don't want to hit it too often. Certain people are prone to certain thresholds because of their wiring. Behavior and the strategies we use are often attempts to manage our threshold.

A nervous system threshold can be different at different times. When you are tired, your threshold for input is lower than at other times. Have you ever noticed that when you are getting sick, you have a shorter fuse? This is because your threshold is so low it is being hit repeatedly, and all these signals bombard the system making you just plain crabby. We might engage in a different manner because our threshold has been hit too often.

- Taking a break, finding some quiet time, or meditation can help someone who has had their threshold hit too often. My daughter tends to have a lower threshold, therefore she doesn't need as much input to reach it and if she does, she might over-respond because there are too many signals.

Sometimes your threshold is impossibly high and it seems you can't do enough to reach it. Now you feel just as bad. We might need more input because of a high threshold.

- Exercise, caffeine, and fidgeting are all strategies that help someone reach a high threshold. I have always been pretty busy, and I need to move a lot to hit my threshold. If I don't reach it, I will have trouble making an appropriate response because there aren't enough signals telling my brain what to do.

There are different ways we can hit our threshold. Most adults have figured out socially appropriate ways to reach their threshold because they have been exposed through the years to different sensory experiences. They are now able to get, *or avoid*, input without disturbing others. Children lack experience and therefore they haven't perfected this skill. The behavior you are seeing might be their attempt to manage their threshold so they can regulate. Is it possible this child is trying to reach their threshold? What if it has been hit so many times that they are now in fight, flight, or freeze. This can look like volitional behavior when really it is simply survival. They may not be able to verbalize it, but they can't do what we are asking of them if they can't regulate.

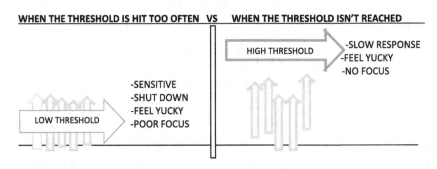

WHEN THE THRESHOLD IS HIT TOO OFTEN VS WHEN THE THRESHOLD ISN'T REACHED

HIGH THRESHOLD
-SLOW RESPONSE
-FEEL YUCKY
-NO FOCUS

LOW THRESHOLD
-SENSITIVE
-SHUT DOWN
-FEEL YUCKY
-POOR FOCUS

The goal is to hit our threshold no matter where it is because then we can regulate.

If it is too low, it gets hit too often. If it is too high, it is hard to reach. Both mean we *cannot* regulate. One child doesn't know they aren't regulated, the other simply *can't*. At the end of the day, neither one is smiling.

My family wiring is busy. We seem to seek out movement, talk more than most, and have trouble sitting still. There are times when I can't focus to save my life. I'm more prone to a little higher threshold, which simply means I need to move a little more, fidget a little more, and exercise is important for me to focus. I know that my wiring affects where my threshold needs are. All of this affects my behavior and the challenges I face with different people or activities. I've never been a quiet, slow-moving creature and probably never will be. But then, a moment arises, and I can't handle anything. It isn't typical, but there are times when the world is just too much. If I am sick or tired, or if for some reason my threshold for stimulation is lower, my performance will be affected very quickly and with much less input. My ability to regulate will be affected by where my threshold is at that moment. This awareness will determine what strategies you will want to use.

DESCRIPTION OF THRESHOLDS

Winnie Dunn created the Sensory Profile. She uses thresholds to describe behaviors we see due to sensory processing issues. The following chart is a quick summary of how I apply her theory and explanation of thresholds and the sensory system. This highlights examples of the behaviors we might see when kids are trying to reach a high threshold, or when they have hit a low threshold too often. You will likely see both high and low behaviors at different times, but these are easy behavioral signs you can use to identify where your child is in order to begin the process of teaching them how to self-monitor.

Affected Sense	High Threshold Behaviors	Low Threshold Behaviors
Touch	- frequently touch people or objects - tend to get into others' personal bubbles - put things in their mouth - chew on shirt or shirt cuffs - display very high pain tolerance	- overreact when people are too close - hate messy things - avoid situations that involve textures they don't like - avoid certain foods - display an overreaction to pain
Taste or Smell	- crave strong, spicy flavors or odors - smells objects that others might not - taste, or put things in their mouth that you wouldn't expect	- avoid flavors or odors more than others and may not know why
Sound	- make noises or talk through and verbally process everything - seek out noises that distract them from what they are doing	- strongly dislike certain noises - startle easily, cover ears - difficulty working in groups - assemblies or lunch cafeteria can be a time of behavioral outburst
Vision	- need a lot of visual stimulation such as with bright lights - continuous distractions from movement or visually stimulating objects like looking out the window, TV, video games	- overstimulated by visual detail - behavioral outburst at the beginning of long homework or work - can't find objects hiding in detail
Vestibular- related to balance and space	- constantly jumping, swinging, bouncing - always drawn to activities involving movement	- car sick, avoid play equipment like swings or slides - poor behavior after transitions that involve bending to get something which tips the head
Proprioception- knowing where your body is, how things feel	- need to crash, push/pull, hit, or bite more than others - play too hard and not understand why peer is hurt by their high-five or tag	- sedentary play choices that are quiet, with little movement - overreact to pain - seems weak with easy activities

HIGH THRESHOLDS: WHEN
THEY CAN'T BE REACHED

High threshold issues are a result of not getting enough signals. Sleepy dragons are the main culprit here, and they are not doing their job. There is nothing to respond to and nothing is even on their radar. More input is needed even to get the child's attention. They may struggle in situations where they must sit for a long time because the threshold isn't reached without movement. They may be desperately trying just to *feel* something, and often they get in trouble during this process.

Regulation is impossible if we can't hit this threshold because it is the threshold that allows our nervous system to react, attend, and begin to understand the signals coming in. Maybe things aren't registering the same way they do for others. There can be an excessive amount of information but still no signals. Sometimes no amount of movement is enough because it takes so much extra input to reach that high threshold.

Irrelevant of *why* this threshold can't be reached, we see the same problem. No regulation. We may be dealing with a kid who has no clue that something needs attention because nothing has registered, therefore they make no response or the wrong response. We may be dealing with a kid who knows something is going on, but can't focus and misses everything. Now we see extreme behaviors because they are attempting to regulate.

A child who is prone to a higher threshold will do all they can to reach it because that is when they feel good. When you say their name five times before they respond, you may assume they are choosing to ignore you. When a child doesn't accurately feel the high-five they just gave a friend, they might hit harder, which usually ends in tears and a time-out. There aren't enough signals, so the behavior isn't appropriate for the situation.

Think of that kid in class who is always distracting those around them with movement, talking, flicking objects for fun. What a stinker, right? But maybe this child is using all this disruption as a way to focus. Sometimes added movement or verbal processing can help kids reach a high threshold but this behavior can be misinterpreted as volitional instead of functional behavior. The goal is to find a way for kids to reach their threshold without disrupting those around them.

EXAMPLES OF HIGH THRESHOLD BEHAVIOR CAN INCLUDE:

- Constantly engaging with the child next to them or picking fights with siblings
- Running their hand along the hallway wall knocking off prized art projects in school
- Hanging on you, the furniture or the dog
- Constant fidgeting, and wiggling in their chair
- Seeking movement, crashing onto the floor or into walls for fun, spinning, rough and tumble play, and loving to swing on the swing set
- Slumping on the desk, unable to start working, looking tired or uninterested because the body can't react unless there is an adequate signal
- Trouble calming down
- Verbal processors are often loud, chatty and constantly talking
- Behavior that appears aggressive. Keep in mind that this assumption of aggression might simply be their attempt to get input because they feel out of control. They can also display seemingly purposeful hitting, pinching, squeezing, grabbing, or pulling because they don't accurately feel what their body is doing when they haven't reached their threshold
- Biting objects or siblings, grinding teeth, or chewing on clothes to the point of making holes in them

- Spinning their body, flapping their hands, and even persistent masturbation can be an attempt to focus or do what is requested
- A high tolerance to pain and touch because information isn't registering
- Trouble with coordination because the brain doesn't know what the body is doing or where it is to adjust

When my son was little, he had a very large and sturdy stuffed lion that was a type of chair or beanbag. It was super cute, but soon I realized it served many more purposes than just somewhere to sit. When he had trouble hitting his high threshold that often resulted in him bowling over his little sister, I noticed he would run and do a lunge, hug, roll maneuver with this lion chair. He sometimes needed to do it two times, but in the end, I realized he had figured out how to get what his system needed to regulate. He eventually figured out that this lion made him feel good and without even realizing it, he had come up with a strategy of his own. This is where the parent detective is so important. Watch what your child goes to in their environment and see what other opportunities can be created in their space.

When signals aren't processed correctly, we might assume kids are behaving poorly by choice.

STRATEGIES TO REACH A HIGH THRESHOLD: INCREASE SIGNALS

- Fidget tools or clay/resistive material to hold or fidget with during listening times will provide heavy input into muscles. Build heavy work strategies into desk or quiet time tasks. Use a resistive band around the legs of the desk or chair so they can push/pull against it with their legs.
- Apply deep pressure down the spine by putting pressure on each shoulder and pushing down.
- Get down on their level, touch their shoulders and look at them.
- Vary sit and downtime with up and movement time.
- Modify the environment. Provide more texture, dynamic seating options, minimize the clutter in a workspace, make space for a safe rumble room for that channeled energy to go somewhere socially appropriate. Provide more

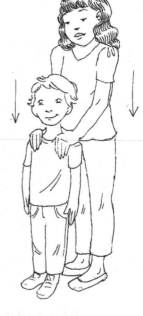

intense and frequent stimulation. Think of all the senses and different ways you can incorporate them into strategies that occur frequently and with more volume, speed, etc. Rocking fast, loud and upbeat music, and movement strategies that occur during an extended activity can help when it is hard to focus. A bell or noise can give a signal to start and stop an activity.
- Use bright paper or binders for subjects that are harder for your child. Try glittery ink, smelly pens, mechanical pencils, pencils or pens with fidget tools on the eraser. These can be purchased or made but are things that go over the eraser that the child can manipulate or fidget with.
- Listen to upbeat music to bring that energy up.

- Set frequent but subtle check-in or chimes that can increase self-monitoring and prompt the question, "Am I focused when the chime goes off?" Apps that help with focus are readily available now, and they even send reminders to see if you are focused at that moment.
- Play and move bodies *before* work. Many people think play time should be after work, but most people need to move their bodies before working.
- Work for 5 minutes, then move. This is an excellent strategy for the toolbox because once you feed the nervous system with movement, it's able to focus clearly and even filter better to complete more work.
- Dynamic sitting options allow and encourage different positions for desk work. Examples include lying on their stomach, standing at a table, sitting on a ball, or writing on the board vs. paper. This dynamic opportunity requires them to make small postural adjustments that feed their nervous system and affect that dragon.

- Sports and exercise can feed the nervous system with effects that can last 2-6 hours. Running, lifting weights, riding bikes, and organized sports are all a vital part of a child's world and will affect their ability to attend to a given activity even after they are done moving.
- Oral input is very organizing. The mouth is like the computer terminal to the brain, and gum can be a useful tool. When you see kids with their fingers in mouth, chewing on their pencils, clothing, or other items, this can be an indication that they do well with oral input. You can buy bracelets, necklaces, and pencil toppers that are designed to be chewed.
- Confirm that they got the instructions. Some look like they aren't listening, but they are. Others may need to look away or doodle to listen. Figure out what works for your child and share this with

their teacher. Some may look you right in the eye and hear nothing while others may fidget or doodle and catch everything!

- A sensory diet is an activity plan designed to regulate a child's threshold. Every child is different, so what works for one may not work for another. The idea is to try an activity and determine if it accomplishes what is needed. Does it give the child the input they need to reach and maintain a calm, alert state that allows them to be successful in the given environment? These activities are called a sensory diet because the input is spread throughout their day and within activities or transitions. Much like needing food throughout the day, we need input to regulate. Full-body exercises such as jumping jacks, pushups, sit-ups, chair pushups, or jobs that involve carrying heavy things like books to the kitchen are legitimate sensory diet tools.

- Heavy work is any kind of activity or job that makes us use our muscles. It usually involves lifting, pushing, pulling, or exercise. Kids can stack chairs, carry books, play hard at recess, or try out a boot camp or teacher's helper vs. staying in at recess. Chair pushups are when you put hands beside your hips and push into the chair to lift feet and bum up off the chair, and hold this position.

LOW THRESHOLDS: WHEN THEY GET HIT TOO OFTEN

When every little thing is noticed, whether from our body or the environment, we say this is a low threshold for input. When we hit our threshold quickly and repeatedly, there are signals everywhere. The signals can be so strong they can stay in the belly or chest, and create that red-in-the-face look we often see with stress and anxiety. The result is usually a meltdown because hitting their threshold too frequently means too many warning signals are bombarding them.

> Think of when you are getting sick. The lights suddenly bug you, noise is unbearable, and even your skin is sensitive.
>
> Our threshold is much lower in this situation.

Some kids feel this yuck and simply respond. Others do everything they can to avoid feeling it at all. The way a child responds to this feeling can differ greatly even though it is still about too many signals and an overreactive dragon. The dramatic reaction we see can be an attempt to avoid any opportunities and they may be in the fight or flight state most of the time because their world is just too stimulating. These kids seem fragile. They have tons of worries. They are sensitive and often emotional or anxious.

Weak? No. Overstimulated? *Yes!*

Remember again how you feel when you are getting sick. The world is just too much, and all you want to do is get under the covers and not come out. The book, <u>Too Loud Too Bright Too Fast Too Tight: What to Do If You Are Sensory Defensive in an Overstimulating World</u> by Sharon Heller is a valuable resource for signal issues and it applies to adults too. When your wiring makes you prone to experiencing the world with too many signals, everything is louder, more intense and *everything* creates stress.

Loud noises, a pat on the back, even a sharp turn while riding in the car can result in over-stimulation and a surge *way past* their threshold.

Trying new foods, new equipment on the playground, new people... none of this has gone well, and it won't go well this time. *No.* There is a battle, and the intensity we see will depend on how this incoming information can be managed. They may have *very* strong preferences, and these must be respected. If we respect their words, they may be able to push through. If we challenge their "no", we may see the fire dragon at its very worst.

EXAMPLES OF LOW THRESHOLD BEHAVIOR CAN INCLUDE:

- Avoiding eye contact because it's too intense
- Always having a hoodie on because this allows them to block out the visual and auditory input and makes a little cave that feels safe
- Wearing headphones to drown out unexpected noise or cancel outside noise
- Being over-sensitivity to touch. They may avoid touch from others and display behavior issues when an activity involves touching textures they don't like. They may hate when their hands are dirty, or not like walking in sand or grass with bare feet. Basic hygiene issues like washing hair, brushing teeth or clipping nails can be hard. Sometimes tolerance to touch is better if the child can initiate the activity because control and anticipation can make this sensation more manageable.
- Sensitivity to noise or loud spaces. They may avoid noise or show extreme behavior in anticipation for a noise they know they can't handle like a public restroom toilet or the hand dryers.
- Managing a day when they don't know what to expect, struggling with transitions or unexpected changes that might seem fun for other kids. Activities like surprises, parties with lots going on, or last-minute changes in the day are not things they generally enjoy.
- Extreme tantrums or motor responses. When kids overstimulate, some respond to counteract what they feel so they might hit themselves in the head or bolt out of the building.
- Poor engagement. Some kids respond with shut down instead of extreme reactions.

- Distractions they create that allow them to avoid a given task they can't handle
- Any unexpected change such as, "It's a substitute teacher today, and she doesn't look fun!"
- Over response to pain
- Over-sensitivity to noise, busy environments, lights, and movement like swings, slides, or car rides

THE "DEAL WITH IT" APPROACH NEVER WORKS HERE!!

STRATEGIES TO DECREASE OR MANAGE SIGNALS WHEN THE THRESHOLD IS TOO LOW

- Heavy work: start with giving the child something to lift or push or pull (proprioception and tactile input). Heavy work and important jobs are pretty safe ways to start, and any time we use our muscles we can usually regulate the signals. Don't put just any kid on a swing (vestibular input) because they may not tolerate this, and you can make things worse.

- *See what the child gravitates toward. Their behavior and preferences can usually tell you exactly what they need!*

- If they do a lot of jumping, spinning, crashing, or rolling, they may need to go to the playground for some vestibular strategies or heavy work.

- If they are hitting, banging their head, or biting, they might need deep pressure. Start with a big squeeze. They can do it to themselves, or you do it from behind; it is up to you, the child, and your relationship.

- If they are always going toward that dark corner, maybe they need less visual input and a cool, dark cave under a staircase, table, or hall closet.

- Control through "dragon talk" allows kids to feel a sense of power when taming their dragon, and sometimes the biggest meltdowns come from a lack of control. Most dragon issues come from not feeling any control within, so building in as much opportunity for the *perception* of control is usually huge! Provide a couple of options for a starting point, but ultimately give them the last say. Ask them what they think they need to do but remember that the brain doesn't work when the dragon has convinced the system it needs to protect. Sometimes the best option is to get a change in scenery to wait for things to calm down, and then come up with some dragon taming ideas with the child taking the lead.

- Visual schedule: I can't say enough about this, especially with cues for what is first, second, etc. This tool helps channel energy and also can give a light at the end of the tunnel that might provide the appropriate motivation to muddle through the stuff that's hard for their system. When they know they get a break after ten math problems it makes the math more manageable.

- Deep pressure into joints, weighted blanket/vest/lap pad, or wrapping in a blanket provides powerful input that is organizing to the nervous system.

- Calming techniques: breathing, walking breaks, linear swinging or rocking, relaxation books and pressure into the upper lip can really help.

- Foster calmness: speak with a low volume and pace, and model slow breathing patterns to help your child realize they have control over their breath.

- Input into jaw muscles: have them eat crunchy or chewy snacks, suck a thick liquid through a straw, chew gum, or suck on hard candies.

- Avoid Fight or Flight. Our protective system kicks in when we have more input than we can integrate. When you notice a child has hit this point, take a deep breath and help them find a quiet place where they can take a break until they can control their body and focus attention. We all need breaks. A quiet or different environment allows the brain a chance to reset.

- Structure: if your child knows the general sequence of the events in their day, they can better anticipate and prepare for it.

- Deep Pressure: push hands together, like trying to squish something, and hold. This is a quiet trick a child can do on their own at school when needed and it creates little distraction.

- Finger fidget tools: this can be made from a rubber band and paper clip, try koosh balls or other balls that they can squeeze tightly, or pencil toppers that allow them to fidget with something while they are listening.

- Provide distractions, or focus on one aspect of an activity that might be silly or fun. This is similar to concepts used in therapy. Kids can be afraid of heights, but when the dragon thinks we are only climbing to find monkeys that are hiding up in the trees, his focus shifts from, "Yikes, this is too high" to, "Where are those pesky monkeys hiding?" The other neat thing about this approach is that the nervous system can often process this new input, which makes it easier the next time it is attempted.

- Look for additional problems such as being sick, tired, hungry, or irritated by a tag in their shirt. These make everything harder and can quickly be addressed once identified.
- Change the environment. Change or add structure, simplify the task, notice and address the physical environment that is distracting such as noise or too much going on around them.
- Provide opportunities for movement or breaks. Some calming strategies that seem to work include heavy and slow lifting, yoga, deep breathing, or anything that allows the senses to essentially exhale.
- Time in the dark, or even dim lighting, is a great way to calm.
- Play detective with your senses. Think about how music can affect us. Have you ever heard that awesome rhythm with fast drums and a catchy tune and just wanted to get up and dance? The same is true for the slower, calmer music... it conjures pictures of fluffy PJ's, curled up on the couch. Think of the sensory aspects right in front of you, right now. Are the lights humming? Are they bright? Is there a TV or radio on? Maybe white noise? Did you burn popcorn? Popcorn seems pretty specific I know, but if you've ever burnt popcorn, you know that obnoxious smell can linger for days. Become the detective and help your child do the same. Try to quiet the dragon enough to look around and change what's right under your nose. You'd be surprised the difference this little bit makes. After that, talk about the toolbox. Help them figure out what might be helpful.
- Sometimes a worry stone they carry in their pocket is enough. Other times, they may need to figure out a way to advocate for their needs, ask for a break to get a drink or to remove themselves from the situation.
- Seat the sensitive child where people don't brush against them.
- Use warm-up activities like stretching, heavy work, or deep pressure.
- Utilize a timer so there is a visual cue showing how much longer to work or attend.

- Warn in advance to allow the child to anticipate intense sensory experiences and discuss ways of preparing for certain noises or environments. Parades, birthday parties or fireworks might be activities that are hard for them to manage without knowing what is involved or what strategies they might be able to try.
- Time-out works for some kids, but if you are dealing with a Tigger, movement and heavy work will be more successful at helping them get back on track.
- Reduce the social aspect. Social skills can create a lot of unknowns. Some kids do better with adults because adult behavior can be more predictable than kids so it is way less scary.
- Create obstacle courses for training dragons that involve movement such as pushing or pulling, and anything heavy that makes the dragon really work.
- Jumping up and down stimulates the vestibular system and provides the heavy impact of proprioception into all the joints and muscles of the body. This utilizes two of the three foundational roots.
- Take out the dragon trash, rearrange furniture, vacuum.
- Hug pillows to keep them fluffy or flat.
- Dragon journals: I use a composition book and have them draw what the dragon looks like. Then we cut out pictures of strategies and put them into a homemade pocket in the front of the book. Now they can choose one or two when they need help. The pages turn into a place where they can draw or write about what worked, what didn't, and what they can try next time. This is especially helpful for the fire dragons that cause lots of worries and anxiety because now it can double as a worry journal too.
- Dragon caves can be constructed and this will also tell you what things they need when they seek comfort and peace. Often this is very different than what we as adults would make for them, so follow their lead.
- Make up games like a fast-food restaurant where you wrap your child in a tortilla blanket, nice and tight. If they'd rather have a burger, you can put on mustard and a bun using couch cushions

with pressure. They have fun but still get heavy, organizing pressure.

- Crawling is a basic pattern for integration of sensory information in the nervous system. Try belly crawling or crawling on all fours.

My son was two and standing in my sister-in-law's kitchen. We were talking about sugar and she mentioned she had seen a study that said sugar doesn't really affect behavior like we thought it did. I grew up in that house with very little sugar. I was intrigued and half hoped my mom had been wrong all these years. I said, "Let's see". My son was borderline out of control at the mere thought of a cookie, but we both sat back to see if the show got better. Suffice it to say, sugar does affect some kids.

For my kid, it caused him to hit his threshold repeatedly until all we were left with was complete mania! On his 5th lap through the kitchen chasing the cat, my sister-in-law agreed that he was sensitive to sugar. Similar to being sensitive to input like we see with a low threshold, the end result was complete chaos… not scary, or mean, just out of control.

HELPING KIDS UNDERSTAND THRESHOLDS

Nervous system thresholds can change throughout the day, throughout life, and with different activities or demands. Problems occur when the *balance* between activity and energy is off. When the threshold is hit too often, or not at all, it can quickly turn into the bull in the china store scenario.

Different activities require different thresholds. If we have a big mountain bike race in 20 minutes, my son is capable of waking up his dragon because this activity creates a lot of input that gets him up to his higher threshold. My daughter knows the race is in 20 minutes too, but she has had signals shooting around for two hours already, and presents very different behavior. She is almost in shut-down mode before the race starts, and my son is only just revving up. Helping them to understand *why* they feel like they do can allow them to better manage their behavior and emotions. My daughter can ignore her excess signals so she can ride her best and focus on fun. My son knows he needs to do more to wake up that dragon for more signals on the trail that keep him safe while going fast.

Bedtime is no different. Does your child spin out of dreamland despite the 8,487 sheep they have counted? Maybe your other child is asleep the minute their head hits the pillow. While thresholds *do* change, you can see how wiring can affect where that threshold usually lies. What can you do to help your child who is still awake at midnight because they are driven by a fire dragon? Sounds like strategy time. Perhaps try some deep breathing while listening to music or a bedtime story. Make sure they weren't watching TV or in front of a screen right before bed. Maybe a warm bath with dim lighting and quiet music will help their threshold to adjust. Your child will know what feels good so make sure to include them in the creation of these ideas. They can start a "sleep journal" to remember the solutions that helped them relax and calm down.

Disney Characters are useful for young children and one of my favorite conversations. Tigger is bouncing all over the place and very prone to a high threshold; he is hard to talk to or play with. Then there's Piglet. He avoids many opportunities because of his low threshold; he is getting fire signals too often, which means he avoids and worries constantly. Pooh is right in the middle. He can eat honey with the best of them, fly kites, chat with friends, climb trees if he needs to… do you see the correlation? Pooh is regulated, Tigger and Piglet are not. Relating to the characters may help your child find safe ways to understand how they are feeling.

Helping your child begin to self-monitor what they are feeling is the first step. Finding something they already love to talk about makes the conversation more relevant and valuable, not to mention motivating. They will likely create the flow once you start the ball rolling, so keeping it at their level and considering their interests will make for fun scenarios!

- Are you having a Tigger moment and missing cues all around you? Maybe your sleeping dragon just won't wake up.
- Are you having a Piglet moment where you just can't seem to function because everything is scary, and you shut down twenty minutes ago? Maybe your fire dragon is shooting flames and making too much noise. Now nothing can be heard, and you definitely can't see through all the smoke!

The use of external characters to start a discussion with your child can make all the difference. Nothing is wrong with them, but something is preventing them from enjoying the situation they are in. Many children also struggle with self-esteem because life is hard, and even when they try, they often can't find success. Dragons and Disney characters are tangible and visual objects that can remove the blame for the moment and give direction for solutions without making it personal.

Think about the various things we do as the regulated adult to anchor ourselves and improve our regulation. All the areas we have discussed to look at for our kids are likely candidates for our own strategies.

- Some people use movement: maybe you tip the chair, bounce your foot, rock, fidget, or pace.
- Proprioception or deep pressure may be what you prefer; can you tell when you don't get your workout? Do you love to be wrapped tight or under heavy blankets?
- Auditory input: do you often have music on or hum to yourself? Do you need white noise to fall asleep or focus?

- Tactile or touch input can be very powerful. Do you twist your hair, click pens, or play with fidget tools... touch and explore different textures?
- Visual input can include watching a fish tank or a water feature. Does the space need to be organized and clutter-free? Is it busy and full of color and stuff?
- Oral input is organizing for everyone. Are you a nail biter or gum chewer? Do you find yourself seeking out crunchy or chewy snacks?

Recognizing what we choose can help us come up with ideas to share with our kids, and at the very least, give us some insight into how frequently we use strategies to regulate. Yours are likely more socially appropriate, but they serve the same purpose for you as for your child.

EXECUTIVE FUNCTIONING: SKILLS

EXECUTIVE FUNCTIONING AND THE BRAIN

I quickly figured out that kids can struggle with signal issues at times, and while sensory strategies can help, they aren't always enough. Sure, it's helpful to reframe, to see the situation differently, and self-monitoring remains critical. But things can still be challenging. At this point I began to dive into the skills and the world of brain development... specifically, executive functioning.

By the time you hit this point in the book, you've probably figured out if your child has a hard time with sensory processing and signals. Maybe you even tried some of the new ideas and had a dragon conversation with your child. What if your child has embraced their wiring, understands the importance of regulation, but is still struggling? Skills which reside in the thinking brain are the other key piece to this puzzle and the *why* of behavior.

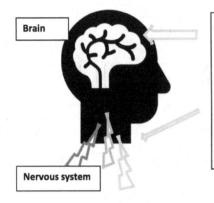

Brain

Executive functioning skills are in the thinking part of the brain and what we use for execution or to make a response.

Signals or sensory information come in from the body and nervous system. They are the connection and communication between our body and our world.

Nervous system

Executive skills allow for flexibility. We need to be able to determine the significance of a situation and make an alternative plan if the first one doesn't work.

Executive functioning is dependent on sensory processing because if we don't get signals, or we get too many signals, the thinking part can't think. Dragons provide us with a way to talk about these signals, but sometimes they are not the problem. Sometimes the signals come in, but the skills are weak, so there is no response or a delayed response. This can quickly look like intentional behavior such as defiance or a lack of motivation, etc. It can be confusing, but just remember the goal... regulation.

Regulation comes with a balance of signals and skills.

- If the signals come in and the skills are strong, we will see regulated behavior.
- If there are few or *no signals*, this can be a high threshold issue or a problem with sensory processing. With no signals, the thinking part can't work even if the skills are strong.
- If there are *too many signals,* like we see with fight or flight, this can be a low threshold issue or problems with sensory processing. Too many signals prevent the thinking part of the brain from working, so it won't matter how strong the skills are; we still can't access them.
- If signals come in, the threshold is hit, and balance is found, the thinking part of the brain should work. But now, what if the needed skill is weak or late to develop so the execution or response

is slow or non-existent? The skills are too low for the demands of the situation. *Now we have a problem.*

Sensory processing and executive functions are inter-dependent.
We need signals and we need skills for regulation.
If you want to know the why of behavior,
you have to be aware of both.

This is how executive functioning can affect the behavior we see, even when everything else seems okay. If we have signal problems *and* executive skill issues, we will see big trouble.

Dragons and thresholds are ways to talk about signals. The two big players for regulation are signals from *sensory processing* and skills from *executive function.*

- Sensory processing is responsible for the signals. We might have a dragon imbalance or a threshold issue so we need to know if the signals are working.
- Executive functions are the doing, the execution, and the production or behavior we expect to see. If these aren't strong, the execution will be affected.

Executive skills aren't the same as cognitive skills, and they aren't related to IQ. They are skills that make it possible to execute or learn from experience. They are like the air traffic control center of our brain, and there are many areas of the brain responsible for the complex behaviors that make us successfully human. They are like any other skill. They must be developed, learned, and then practiced. They are the foundation for navigating the demands of childhood, and eventually the complexities of adulthood.

Remember watching your child learn to walk? They would stand at the table forever. Maybe smiling, maybe fussing, but standing and standing. Maybe they rocked side to side, perhaps they let go for a moment. We encourage, anticipate, and cheer on the process of walking. We would never expect our infant to walk without first watching, standing, getting stronger, and eventually practicing. Expecting the behavior and skills that come from brain development is no different than the process of walking.

We rejoice in our child's first steps. Walking is a skill that comes with development, practice, and **TIME.**

Walking is a milestone. Executive skills are too!

They are developmental skills that we master with practice, and over time they allow us to execute effectively.

WHY EXECUTIVE FUNCTIONING MATTERS

Much of my job as an occupational therapist is to figure out intense behavior, especially with kids. These intense behaviors are tough for everyone, even the amazing psychologists, counselors, social workers, and administrators I work with. Neuroscience has come a long way, and there are many studies and scans that support theories of brain development and behavior. There are parenting approaches that focus on tough love and fear-based motivation. If you have tried these and behavior has not changed, that's probably why you are reading this book. It's time to try something else.

It became apparent that the process of *why* and *how* was likely at the root of behavior and regulation. As a parent, I am always trying to find anything that will work with my kids, and let's not forget that what works for one kid often doesn't work for the other. Individual wiring, signals, and skills are all relevant to what actually works. We also can't forget that what works one day might not the next. *Yuck!*

I also quickly learned that my expectations can influence whether or not my child can find success. The success a child finds in reaching expectations and demands of a situation is directly related to skills and signals. When there is an imbalance that prevents regulation, the difference between this child's ability and their potential can be huge. When the expectations or demands are so much higher than the signals or skills of the child, we generally see maladaptive behavior such as frustration, shutdown, distractibility and failure. When this gap is too big to overcome, we have not presented the just-right-challenge.

> **When the demands of a situation exceed the skills of the child, behavioral regulation is hard.**

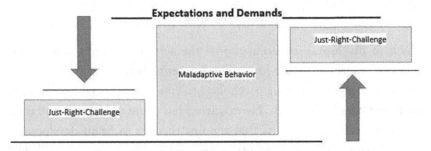

Child's ability **Signals **Skills**

This is a wonderful opportunity for intervention. If there is something we can do to affect the signals or skills we will narrow this gap. When a child is struggling, there is little in the moment that will impact the signals and skills, so we must address our expectations or the demands of the situation. This can mean using fewer words, writing a list in addition to telling them the list, or giving them additional time to respond. Only when this gap narrows and the just-right-challenge is presented, will a child find success. Only then, should we increase our expectations and demands... never before.

> Holding our child to expectations that might be appropriate for a peer or even younger siblings doesn't necessarily mean they are appropriate for this child and their developmental ability.
>
> Respect for this timeline allows the child to try without judgement, fail without fear, and gain knowledge from experience. Everyone fails and everyone gets scared, sometimes.
>
> Everyone must learn to recover.

If adults are stressed by the struggle their child is facing, it will affect how they engage with this child. Anxiety and the resultant lack of regulation also affects adults. When kids are dealing with an adult who is stressed, they will act like a sponge and soak up all that stress. Being aware of how we are responding may give us tips that explain why our child is responding as they are. If we are scared, they likely will be too. If we are stressed or anxious, the energy of that space actually changes.

IT IS ALL ABOUT PERSPECTIVE

When we look at this child who truly can't find success, it is difficult to help if we don't figure out the *real* problem... in *their* world. Maybe it is something at school, or an issue with the kids next door. Perhaps they don't even realize there is a problem until it is too late. We must remember to involve them in the process of problem solving. As adults, it is hard not to tell kids what is going wrong from *our* perspective and it is even harder to not tell them what to do.

What we need is *their* perspective. We can make observations or guesses, but reminding your child that he or she is the expert here can be empowering and motivating. We can't care more than they do about *their* problem, and we certainly can't assume to understand more about it than they do. Perspective is something that isn't always accurate, and that is why they still need you. They need to process and execute, and providing your insight is critical to helping them realize an accurate perception. When we don't hear their side or perspective, we might be missing the one opportunity to see the big picture. We can guide them, even share with them, but theirs is the only perspective that will forever be guiding them.

Executive skills are brain-based behaviors involved in just about everything we do. If the doing or lack of doing is the problem, executive functioning needs a serious look. What do weak executive skills look like? Here are just a few things that you might be experiencing with your child that are related to executive skill development:

- Interrupts conversations regularly
- Doesn't follow through with tasks like homework or chores
- Talks or plays too loudly and shows impulsive behavior
- Bedroom or locker is a disaster with no organization of anything
- Always late, has trouble with time and use of time
- Difficulty learning from experience, so the same mistakes are made over and over
- Trouble with sustained attention and effort

- Behavior regulation issues or trouble analyzing a situation and adjusting behavior
- Difficulty with flexibility when the schedule or activity changes
- *Starting* a task that isn't preferred. Legos are very different than homework.
- Poor self-monitoring, prioritization, and goal-setting ability
- Writing is disorganized, work is messy, and very few words make it on the page
- Behavior is often described as unmotivated, lazy, not interested, bored, hyperactive, distracted, typical teen, etc.

I was *that mom* who was always one step ahead of my child. I would get everything ready for them to grab on the way out the door. No one would be late; they would always have everything they needed. The problem is, my kids never had to execute because I did it all for them. My doing too much prevented them from perfecting their executive functioning skills like planning and organization. Sure, mine were getting better by the day, but this was not my goal!

We went away for the weekend, as we had so many times before, and my son was packing his own bag. He brought one pair of socks. I don't know what your kid's feet smell like, but suffice it to say, extra socks are a good thing! It never really occurred to him during packing that he might need multiple pairs. In past trips, he always reached into his bag, and there they were... plenty of socks! Now we all got to experience the natural consequence of his poor planning! Long weekend!

When an adult steps in every time a child needs to *get ready*, the skill of planning and then *execution* might not have the chance to develop. Like walking, if a child is always carried and never gets to walk on their own, they won't figure it out on their own. If you plan something and plans change, can you adjust? Do your kids just go along for the ride? When kids don't practice or plan they won't be good at executing or adjusting to change.

When my kids got older and I began working more, I was shocked at how hard it was for them to execute. They struggled with their schedule, timing their morning routine, and even remembering essential items they needed all the time. It is important to remember that when we structure every moment of our kids' lives, whether they are wonderful and enriching activities or not, we take away the brain development that stems from being bored. And it is really important to remember that play is just as important as piano lessons, sports and even school.

There is a reason that *play* is fun… it is joyful, motivating, and sometimes even safely unpredictable. It's also the most important job we can undertake to ensure adequate brain development. Think of all those incredible things that happen during play: touching different textures, making up new games with exciting and ever-changing rules, moving our bodies. We try things out with friends only to discover they don't like the idea. Now we have to compromise and adjust and even reinvent. These are only a few of the things we encounter with play. Even as adults, experiences that involve more peer interactions and planning of events, and the changes required when things don't work, are all skills that our brain must regularly manage.

Video games and all the fun and excitement that come with television and movies don't force us to come up with the ideas, planning, and input that the brain needs to fully develop. Forming letters out of Play-doh or writing them in shaving cream involves many more areas of the brain than using a pencil and paper or using a computer mouse. Requiring that coloring projects look just like the example limits the opportunity and various areas of the brain necessary to complete that project. These are all foundational activities that help to develop executive skills for both home and school.

EXECUTIVE FUNCTIONS

THE DETAILS AND WHY THEY AFFECT BEHAVIOR

- **Executive skill development for tasks like goal setting and problem-solving tends to peak at 16-18 years with full maturation at 25. ALL children need to develop these skills.** Executive skills improve with practice and development. All kids have underdeveloped executive skills because their brains are still maturing. I remember watching as my toddler finally figured out how to move the stool over to the fridge to reach the cookies that were perched above. This was a true feat of *execution*! Developmentally, he was now able to use a tool to help him achieve the end-goal of getting a cookie, and he was able to plan through the multiple steps required to meet that goal. He couldn't have done it before because those parts of his brain weren't ready. He would soon do it in a more complex manner because he was now mastering something that he would be extremely motivated to practice and ultimately perfect.

  But if this is true, why do some adults also have trouble with some of the many skills related to executive functioning? There are disorganized adults and those who can never arrive on time and these are all symptoms related to executive skills. Keep in mind that they are *skills*, so learning and perfecting them will require practice. Just because my adult brain is fully developed doesn't mean I am good at all these skills.

- **Executive skills are worse when a child is stressed, tired, or has sensory issues.** The child's wiring and threshold will affect behavior and their tolerance for everything. If a child is tired, stressed, or out of sync with their threshold, their brain won't work to full capacity. Guess where all the executive skills lie? Yes, in the brain. Poor signals mean there will be no way to execute or demonstrate any of the skills that may or may not be mature. If they have a dragon issue and reside in the world of fight or flight, the brain doesn't work either. If they don't get any cues from the dragon, they can miss key things related to acceptable behavior and the skills may not even be attempted.

- **Executive skills develop in the brain, and dopamine is a neurotransmitter that helps to motivate us and it determines what is worth *doing*!!** You know how your child can *play* for hours on end, even if they can't seem to focus for longer than 10 minutes at school? Play is motivating... work is *not*! This is where some of our brain chemicals can really help us out. Think of what you enjoy about the end of the day. For me, it is my comfy sweats and a glass of wine. When I'm looking at a pile of laundry or a sink full of dishes, I imagine the end. I know when all the jobs of the day are done, I can exhale and indulge in *my* time. Kids are no different. Building in a motivator is vital to helping this child.

    We have receptors in our brain that respond to dopamine and signals then tell the brain to respond. When there is not enough dopamine, which is especially common in the teenage years and with kids who are diagnosed with an attentional deficit, it is hard to get through non-preferred tasks. Video games produce considerable amounts of dopamine that suddenly isn't there when you ask your child to read a book or finish homework. How can dopamine be released with homework when they're used to the fun and excitement of gaming? If they can focus on what they can do after this not-so-fun task, maybe they can get it done. This is likely why many parenting approaches use rewards for motivation; they are a great substitute until our brain chemicals can take over, and this comes with experience, development, and time.

- **Socially, executive skills are critical because they allow us to calm inappropriate behaviors, read the room and our friends, and begin to understand a situation of non-verbal communication.** If a child runs into a quiet classroom from a loud, busy recess and doesn't adjust their activity level, they will likely get in trouble. If a child is working with a peer and they don't know how to read non-verbal communication, they might not realize that their friend doesn't like people in their bubble, or that they can't handle loud voices. Your child might be delightfully fun and friendly, but if they can't read the room and adjust, they may struggle socially. Take notice of pre-school kids. They dart right into your personal bubble, often touch you with gooey hands, might snuggle in or try to kiss you with a green, runny nose, and then run away as quickly as they came. Can you imagine if an adult did that to you? This doesn't usually happen because as we develop, so does the skill of reading the room, reading your friend, etc. With some kids, this skill may develop later, and this can be tough in school or with peers. Kids are known for telling it like it is, and this can be a harsh reality if your child struggles with this executive skill.

- **A lack of executive functioning skills can make behavior appear intentional.** This negatively impacts self-esteem, and eventually motivation toward success. This is one of the biggest hurdles I find. When kids aren't working to their potential, they can be called lazy or unmotivated. When they don't jump right into work, we assume it is because they simply don't want to and are *choosing* not to work. When they continue to misbehave, we might assume they are defiant. While this can certainly be the case with all of us at times, it is important to think about the various executive functioning skills that are in demand for a situation. Simply said, if we are asking for more than the child has regarding skills, there will be poor execution. If kids could, they would.

People don't choose to fail. They fail because they don't have the skills or the signals.

They may develop patterns or habits of behavior as a result of lacking skills. Still, at the very beginning when they were first presented with a problem, maybe they never found success because they weren't ready or didn't have the skills or available strategies.

This is why we need a *different lens* to help us see what is actually going on. Before labeling behavior, try to figure out what is required for the situation and determine if they have those skills. Talking to them about this process can be very beneficial because if they can begin to see what is required, it will improve their self-monitoring. Do they have what it takes to do this? They will be better equipped to self-advocate when they realize they are missing a critical component needed for the activity. If you are missing an essential Lego piece, your finished product will look very different. This situation is no different.

Teenagers are especially challenging in this area because they are older, more experienced, and their brains are more developed. It's hard not to have high expectations about their ability, behavior, and skill sets.

- Why aren't they doing what you asked?
- Why are they going so slow? Don't they know we are in a hurry?

Try to consider the executive skill required in what you are demanding. Is it possible that a skill weakness is contributing to their response? Often a simple request involves *several* skills that are all driven by the brain so there is a lot of opportunity for mishap.

- Maybe they are still processing the request. Did you know that it can take 3-5 seconds to process an oral instruction… that is a *really* long time when you are waiting for an answer!
- Maybe they can't plan through the steps to complete the activity.
- Maybe they don't know how to start. Perhaps there is no motivator or dopamine, so they don't have the energy to start.

- **Behavioral challenges: a form of developmental delay?** If kids had the skills to do what was requested, don't you think they would? Developmental delays are defined as an issue that affects function because things don't mature and work when they should. There is a delay. When executive skills are under-developed, this is delayed brain development. Kids don't like to be in trouble and no one feels good when success is hard to find. If kids could succeed, they wouldn't have to listen to nagging, they wouldn't lose privileges, and they would make us happy. If kids struggle with flexibility and adaptability, they can't adjust when the situation changes, so they may melt-down. If they lack frustration tolerance, even little things are hard to move past or overcome. If they have weak problem-solving skills, they can't come up with an alternative to a boring situation, so instead they may whine and complain. This is another way that I have had great success with that silly dragon; he doesn't always have all the skills to get through a situation smoothly, and guess who is in trouble again?

"PLAYING SCHOOL"

SIGNALS AND SKILLS

One of the best ways to help kids is to try to find the *why* of behavior. Behavior is so telling and relevant to success… especially in school. We can quickly walk into a classroom and see which kids can play school and which clearly cannot. However, what we can't see as easily is the intelligence

and potential a child possesses. If a child is struggling and acting out, we assume they don't *want* to be compliant. Maybe they don't have the intelligence. Perhaps the parents are never home to teach them manners. Maybe they are spoiled and always allowed to do what they want at home. Maybe they are *lazy*.

In the book, <u>Lost at School</u>, Ross W. Greene says, "Kids do well *if they can*." This is very different than the assumption, "Kids do well if they *want* to." He compares these two mindsets to demonstrate that our perspective will change how we see behavior and how we handle behavior. When kids don't meet our expectations, is it because they don't want to? Wouldn't all kids behave if they actually *could*?

So why don't they? This seems to be the million-dollar question. How can we help them? How can we motivate them? Is there something about this fast-paced world, especially the academic world, that is preventing them from meeting our expectations? Do you remember the expectations when you were in school? I do, and they were very different than those for my child in school today. Is his brain even ready for this? Can he handle this?

When signal or skill issues exist, playing school can be challenging. Whether signal issues are because of sensory processing deficits, or because a child's wiring makes them prone to threshold issues, there is still a huge problem that needs to be figured out. There are also skills that aren't developed yet, so this student seems distracted, lazy, or defiant. We see this when kids are bright but not working to their potential. Gifted and talented programming in schools is designed to deal with this brain type, yet the maladaptive behavior we often see has to do with expectations that are too high for the specific skills we are asking them to perform. They can do math, but they really can't read the room.

Advocating for your child is critical because signal and skill issues are very much invisible to the uneducated eye. If your child is sitting there with a broken leg, it would be obvious that they can't run the field. Sensory processing issues and executive functioning weakness can be challenging for parents because many people believe this child's behavior is a choice. Many have never heard brain-based explanations to behavior so when a parent attempts to explain *why* their child behaves as they do, it can appear as if they are making excuses.

It can be hard to help your child's teacher and the school understand this behavior and the possible explanations for your child's struggle. It is a very real problem that may or may not be visible at school. If they aren't doing homework, is it because you didn't put your foot down? Or did they sit there for four hours and not even start a problem? You can model to your child how to use words to remedy an unbearable situation that makes learning hard. We are driven first and foremost to survive, so when life gets hard, fight or flight mode takes over, and this can be a real game-changer if it happens regularly at school.

> How do you support your child in school when playing school isn't designed for movers or when it's too noisy or intense to support learning for how they're wired?

SENSORY SIGNAL ISSUES IN SCHOOL

Expectations at school are different. The social aspect of school is more complicated, and kids act very differently at school than at home. Often a parent's report is different than what a teacher sees. This doesn't mean the child isn't struggling at school, nor does it mean that home or school is to blame. It comes down to expectations and a child's ability to reach these expectations at school. Every part of their social and academic life can be affected if they have difficulty achieving or maintaining appropriate arousal levels or regulation for given tasks. When there are too many or too few signals, all they may get is the buzz of the overhead lights or difficulty focusing when the teacher is talking. Failure can quickly ensue from nearly impossible expectations to finish a project, copy from the board, or work in a group with peers. And now it's time for the very best of all… to socially navigate recess and lunch! It's no wonder our kids can't sit down and do homework when they get off the bus!

There is a big difference between bad behavior and sensory overload. When a child gets over-stimulated, overwhelmed, or can't focus when their peers can, it affects not only their nervous system responses and behaviors but also their self-esteem. When teachers or parents can help children understand the dragon sitting at their desks, they can help teach them to self-monitor and pick up on times when their dragon just won't relax or wake up.

- Strong sensory preferences can be hard to control or navigate when the comforts of home aren't possible at that moment. Snacks, quiet spaces, and a comforting hug might not be possible at school. If these are things required for regulation, school behavior will be tough to manage.
- Focused attention is critical for school and this requires regulation. Thresholds affect our ability to feel good and regulate.

o   High thresholds may require more movement to reach, but what if this is hard to do in the classroom? What if the teacher doesn't understand the need for movement, and your child doesn't know they need to move to help them focus? What if your child can't explain *why* they always get out of their chair?

o   Low thresholds are at risk of being hit over and over in a class with lots of noise, movement, colors, and smells. Everything can cause the threshold to be hit way too quickly.

A lot can be done in the school setting to help a child with signal issues succeed and enjoy their academic years. Much of this has to do with understanding that the sensory world controls just about everything related to regulation.

Kids may demonstrate behaviors that appear disruptive, disrespectful, or disorganized. What you see may just be their attempt to find success, and they might be trying very hard to fit in... they just need some help.

It's often not a conscious thing they can put into words, but they can feel it. You can see it in their behavior. You may even see it for the entire walk to the Principal's office. It will reflect the way they wrote the paper and how they interact with their friends. Even kids who actually make bad choices have likely done it out of necessity at some point. Behavior is tricky, and while consequences are critical for molding behavior, helping a child figure out the role their dragon is playing can be a crucial step for molding behavior too!

Time to talk about the dragon. Is it acting like there is something truly dangerous lurking around the next corner? What could it be? Hmmm.... let's stop for a moment. What can we do? Deep breathing? Water break? A little time in a quieter space? Good! Now... what lurks around the corner of the dreaded 2nd grade wing? What???!!! Nothing??!! Interesting!

Silly Dragon!

Can you imagine what it's like to be different from others but have no idea why? What if the simplest of things felt painful, but weren't interpreted as painful by anyone else? What if you looked around the room only to discover everyone is almost done with their assignment, but you have barely started and actually can't even remember the instructions? What if the tag in your shirt bugged you so much that you yelled at your friend when he asked to borrow a pencil? Now you sit in the corner, by yourself, waiting for that lecture again? What if you are playing a game of tag on the playground, but when you go to tag your friend, you hit them *way* harder than you meant to? Now everyone thinks you hurt him on purpose, and your good friend is hurt.

- Too many signals mean your child may feel too much, respond too quickly, and feel uncomfortable with most everything. They usually create habits or display behaviors as a way of avoiding certain activities, clothes, or experiences. Their nervous system doesn't perceive the input correctly, and everything puts them into protection mode.
- Too few signals means your child doesn't feel enough, process enough or fast enough, and it is almost like they are in a bubble.

They usually get in trouble because they did something with good intentions, but it didn't turn out as they thought it might.

Whether there are too many or not enough signals, the result seems the same. This child is in trouble, again. Welcome to fight or flight... again. Unfortunately, their attempts at playing school or use of strategies can look like misbehavior because they genuinely don't understand the *how* or *why*. One of the biggest successes is helping parents, teachers, and caregivers understand that the signal imbalances are very real to the child, not always something the child makes up to get attention.

THE SCHOOL ENVIRONMENT

While we don't have a direct impact on what happens in the school environment, we need to understand how this can affect our child and their behavior at school. Modifying or changing an individual's environment can be critical to treating the problem. Depending on the child, it can include reducing or increasing what's going on in a space. If more input is needed, it can involve adding additional light, incorporating movement into activities, or doing more hands-on tasks that increase engagement. If less input is required, it can mean sitting in a spot outside the circle, taking frequent breaks, or having conversations *outside* class about what the child thinks might help them.

When we can adjust features of the environment, behavior can change and life often gets easier. It can take a lot of work at first, but it almost always pays off in the end. Maybe we need to move a desk away from the door. Perhaps a student can carry the teacher's books during an otherwise difficult transition to music class. Even changing where a child stands in line can sometimes make all the difference.

Again, it is important to look at what the child is drawn to or avoids. Suddenly you see the things that their system is either craving or avoiding. Often discussing the dragon scene is quite telling because when a child is asked if they see anything in the classroom that is affecting their dragon, it also opens their eyes to what might really be affecting them. This is the key to regulation.

Regulation begins with self-monitoring. Self-monitoring requires scanning the environment and also inside the body to determine what is going on. The sad thing about our fast-paced educational system is that teachers are ultimately graded by the test scores of their students, so this quickly and often inadvertently becomes the focus of education. At the end of the day, if a child can't regulate, they aren't going to be able to learn anyway, so regulation needs to be a primary objective in how we educate our kids.

Awareness of the learning environment involves observing the visual space, the noise level, and even the schedule. Social and peer interactions are a big part of the environment. When kids are trying to learn *and* navigate social situations, this can quickly become too much, and learning can be very challenging. Welcome to fight or flight… again. Behavioral meltdown is a symptom that something isn't working. The environment is a huge part of intervention, so shifting the focus to include this can often be empowering and quite successful and something you can share with your child's teacher.

Having a dragon chat with the whole family has been very beneficial for my younger clients and even helps parents see a struggle they might not have identified before. Older kids respond really well to the conversation of signals and skills. Either way, I've noticed that when kids begin to understand the why of behavior, they are more accepting of each other. Even little kids can appreciate that there are many kinds of dragons, and *everyone* has to deal with them at one time or another. I guess we are all more alike than we thought! What a nice thing to embrace during childhood. Helping kids to understand we are all in this together and that even Mom might need some strategies, can be very empowering. Sounds like we just taught another life skill!

I worked with an amazing teacher who wanted to try the dragon taming lesson and strategies with her entire class. We made a chart that showed strategies for fire dragons and strategies for sleepy dragons. She showed them pictures to help them begin figuring out what dragon they were dealing with and how to quietly get the input they needed.

One day she came into class, completely overwhelmed and a bit frazzled. She felt a little hand on hers, and looked down only to find one of the toughest kids in her class helping her figure out which strategy would make her dragon feel better!

What an amazing teaching moment!

She was able to see that what she had shared with the class really worked. A student who rarely found success in school was able to help her and be her hero!

The entire class was able to see that *even adults* struggle with dragons and we can all help each other out!

Thank you, Lisa Holland!

IDEAS FOR TEACHERS

Your child's teacher has likely noticed that certain things are hard when dragons show up. Sharing information about what you are doing at home can help them better understand your child, but also give them some ideas for ways to manage times when dragons come to school.

> Sometimes there will be a student who is really hard to teach. These kids are clearly not learning, and figuring out how to help them can, and probably should, look different at times. Making everyone look the same isn't realistic or practical. Don't worry about making all things equal. We need to provide differentiated instruction as much as we can.
>
> Set up a space in the back of the classroom that allows this student to be able to listen if they want, control what they watch, but ultimately still learn. This can be a desk with a partition in front of it, a sheet over a table with a learning space under the table, or a see-through net that is hung and provides a sort of dragon den for these breaks. Obviously, how you choose to create this space will be determined by the age of your student, but just the separation can be very effective.

Teachers today are often dealing with an array of different kids from moment to moment, so coming up with the *why* and *how* is often challenging for even our best educators. There are many ways to help our children when dragons show up at school, and sharing with the teacher how your child reacts at these times can be a great start. When your child is in fight or flight, are they more likely to fight or shut down? Helping other adults in their world understand the why of a child's behavior can make it easier for them to also understand how they can help.

When a child is throwing items and hitting kids in line, we tend to treat them very differently than the child who goes into the bathroom and never comes back or the one hiding under the table in the corner. It is normal for people to get angry and impatient when they are dealing with intense behavior versus shut-down behavior, but the source of the problem is the same for both… regulation. When adults understand that kids are doing the best they can with the signals and their skills, they tend to be more open to helping.

- When a consequence is needed, try an exercise break instead of recess. They still get movement but free time play is what they have lost.
- Try heavy work such as erasing the board, stacking chairs, carrying lunch bags, or running errands for the teacher. Quiet desk time can be addressed by wrapping a TheraBand, or resistive tubing, around the legs of the desk or chair so they can push, pull, or bounce their feet on it as they work.
- Position kids in line for transitions according to their needs. Kids that don't like unexpected touch might do better in the front or back vs. the middle of the line where kids could bump them from all sides.
- Give them items or fidgets to carry or jobs to do during transitions through the hall. For instance, have them count how many specific letters they can find on their walk, bring heavy books to music class, or count how many steps it takes to get to the library, etc.
- Discuss and demonstrate that everyone has a bubble of one size or another. This can give a visual for why some kids get agitated or aggressive when people come too close and get in their bubble.
- Headphones or noise-canceling options such as earplugs or hoodie sweatshirts can help distract and block out unexpected noises.
- Seat buddies can help share notes and make focusing easier because they provide a good example and peer motivation.
- Don't demand eye contact or verbal responses. Allowing kids to feel out a situation before jumping in can prevent fight or flight. We need to pick our battles. Calling on a student to come to the front of the room to do a demonstration in front of everyone might defeat the academic purpose you are trying to achieve.
- Let them rearrange or push furniture, such as a chair with books for weight, around the room. They can also push on the wall to make it straighter like with a wall push-up.

- Weighted lap pads are versatile options because kids can put them on their shoulders or lap, but they can also carry them down the hall, lifting them up and down to work their muscles.
- Use essential oil diffusers to add smells that are alerting and or calming. Kids can decide which scent they prefer and move to that part of the room.
- Add texture or things to touch when they are reading or thinking. You can put Velcro under the desk in little pieces that can be spread in random places for them to find with their fingers.
- Oral anything is good for focus. Gum, water bottle with a straw, and snacks like salty, sweet, or chewy, are ways to improve focused attention.
- Make sure all fidget tools or any other things a child might use to improve regulation are used as tools, *not toys*. Baoding balls are metal balls that have a chime as they are rolled in the hand.
- Share positive strategies for transition times. Have them put a hand on their belly and see if they can feel it going out and in as they breathe. Maybe they count the number of times they breathe from class to the library. Now they are calmer, potentially more focused, and able to monitor their breathing.
- Dynamic sitting options can include:
  - Use of a standing desk: Bed risers or PVC pipe can be used to make desks tall enough to stand for work. They sell standing desks that are wonderful but expensive, so this is an excellent way to see if it will work in your setting before the financial commitment.
  - Floor desk: Lower legs can be taken off of tables and desks to create a floor desk that allows kids to sit on the floor to write or work.
  - Stomach time: Dry erase boards and clipboards make lying on your stomach possible for writing time, and any time we get into this position where our neck is extended it improves our focus. This position is similar to when you are looking up at the ceiling vs. down at the floor.

o   Sitting on a large yoga ball or wobble cushion provides subtle movement, and the cushion can also be used for floor time.

o   Rocking chairs that sit on the floor provide back support and dynamic movement during sitting (Howda or Therm-A-Rest camping chairs are examples). These can also be rolled up and easily used in other places.

o   Allow the child to stand in the back or arrange seating away from distractions.

EXECUTIVE SKILL ISSUES IN SCHOOL

Brain development is something that affects everything that ultimately determines behavior: planning, reading the emotions of others, managing frustration, seeing your involvement in a situation, taking responsibility for your actions, or starting a task that might not be very fun. All of these are skills that involve numerous parts of the brain, and sometimes these areas develop at different times than they might for a peer or a sibling. Sometimes we will see issues that surprise us. All of these issues may impact your child's ability to play school.

- They may be great readers, but if they have no friends, they probably don't care about being a successful student.
- They may have an amazing affinity for math, but if they always forget a pencil or whiteboard to work on in class, they miss valuable instruction that the teacher is providing.
- When kids struggle with the many skills involved with being a successful student and playing school, they must also be able to demonstrate what they have learned. It is really hard to show what they know when the teacher never sees any homework.

The life of education can be a very long road if your child isn't wired to play school. One of the first and most critical skills a child must possess for school is the ability to start a task that might not be fun. Surely my child could navigate second grade work, right? But you can't navigate work if you never start an activity that doesn't look like it will be fun; he loves fun after all!

Second grade. Lots of tears, no smiles, constant stomach aches and nightly conversations about how to make school fun. I tried, yet again, to figure out how I could help him. I volunteered in his class thinking I would be able to see why he hated school. He mentioned that he had a hard time focusing, but there was something more. I had ruled out or addressed any sensory issues I had seen. But it wasn't until we took him out of school for a week's vacation that I began to see a little more of the true picture. Second grade didn't normally involve a lot of homework, but when we took him out of school for a week and brought all the busy work, handouts, new lessons and reading assignments with us, it was clear that this was not going to end well.

I thought I had done everything to prepare my son for school, and he loved to learn. This school thing should be amazing! *Wrong again*!

You may have a child who simply *cannot* behave at school. You may have a kid who can fake it for a while, but usually they hit a wall as the academic world gets harder or the social piece gets more complicated. As responsibilities increase, so does the difficulty. When this happens, executive skill weaknesses are often a big part of the problem. If you have had a meeting with your child's teacher to discuss how they are struggling with behavior or work production and nothing is changing, perhaps you need a different approach. Your child isn't trying to misbehave. They aren't avoiding the work by choice. It is because their executive skills are preventing the brain from responding to the signals and this makes school, and life, really hard.

When children struggle to organize, do homework, hand in homework, use a planner, or perform in school, we quickly see that this child needs help! School is tough for certain kids who are wired in a way that makes it hard for them to focus, follow-through, initiate or organize their world. These kids can be exceptionally smart but not working to their potential.

Educators and lawmakers always talk about our educational system and how we can keep up with the rest of the world from an educational standpoint. Children today are being pushed and challenged with so much more than I ever remember as a child. Legislation drives curriculum to advance faster. Skills I remember from second grade are now part of kindergarten lesson plans. Young kids today are reading short books, writing full words and short sentences, and this is the norm for today's kindergarten students. These skills are expected at younger and younger ages whether these kids are ready or not.

Play-doh, shaving cream, large diameter pencils and Lincoln Logs are still in some kindergarten classes today and these are important for foundational learning skills. We can still push kids to learn more, read and write more and simply do more and this isn't necessarily a bad thing as long as the foundational types of learning and *play* are also prioritized. The brain will develop, but there will be problems that show up later when academics get harder if the foundational skills are lacking. Just being aware of the importance of these foundational skills and how brain development and executive skills affect school will help you come up with activities that improve learning.

> The dilemma is that child development and
> *brain development* only occur so fast.
>
> We can teach skills and habits, but we also must remember
> the importance of a solid foundation for life-long learning
> which can be missed when the game moves too quickly.

Executive functioning skills *will* affect your student and their success with school. Think of the many skills that are required for good grades, good study habits, and even the social demands of school. Regulation can be severely impacted when executive functioning skills are weak or late to develop, and this affects attention. The other thing to remember is that some skills will be excellent while others are frighteningly non-existent. Smart kids are held to high expectations because their teachers see cognitive potential. However, they don't know *which* skills aren't quite there yet and how this might hinder their performance. We can't be good at everything, and when we are talking about brain development, things mature at different times. Smart kids can have a tough time processing or organizing, so what the teacher sees may be very unlike what your child means to display.

Grades are a big area affected when executive skills are lagging. Grades are designed to show mastery and content knowledge, but when your child's grade doesn't reflect their knowledge, we have to look at the *why* all over again. Consider how executive skills impact these results. Sometimes kids will receive a grade that is affected by more than mastery of the material. When kids are disorganized, they may have trouble remembering to get, do, or hand in homework. What if they are supposed to show mastery in the form of an essay? Now we are asking for much more than content knowledge… we are requiring many more executive skills. There are many ways these skills impact how your child does with school, and understanding their role in the academic process will help you come up with ways to support, coach and teach these skills so life can get a little easier.

HOW EXECUTIVE SKILLS IMPACT PLAYING SCHOOL

- **Organization, planning, and time management** all impact success at school. These three skills will affect *everything* a child does at school and will drive their behavior in every unsuccessful moment. Consider these scenarios:

  • A kid gets to his locker but can't plan where he is going, what is next, what he will need when he gets there, and what he needs to do right now. He will likely be late, marked tardy and probably won't have what he needs in order to interact successfully in class.

  • A kid gets to his locker, piles of stuff come tumbling to the floor and now he spends the entire passing period shoving it all back in. No way did he figure out what he needed or even find it in his organized chaos.

  • A kid thinks that he has enough time to run to his locker after planning the weekend with a friend, only to hear the bell ring as he is working the combination.

  • A kid thinks he has enough time to complete an assignment, but when he realizes he forgot another activity he hadn't written down, he can't focus on this one, so he doesn't complete either assignment. Welcome to fight or flight... again.

  • A kid doesn't accurately monitor his time during a test so he doesn't complete it which impacts the teacher's impression of his content knowledge.

  • A kid who struggles to write, spends 90% of his time on the essay portion of a test only to run out of time and not answer the easy multiple-choice questions.

  • A kid doesn't know how to prioritize so he studies the wrong material.

All of these scenarios will affect our perception of their behavior. Are they lazy? Did they not listen? Do they not care about school? They are late to class again without any materials. If there are too many signals, this kid can't problem-solve through any of these scenarios to find success. If there are no signals, this kid doesn't even know that they should. If skills aren't developed for the demands of the situation, the signals become irrelevant. No response is made that is appropriate, and this child has failed… again.

This might affect their grade and usually the teacher's impression of the effort this child is willing to put forth for that class. Maybe they just ran out of time because of bad planning and delayed skills development.

- **Writing issues. Of all the academic tasks, writing requires the most executive skills!** There is usually a length requirement of five paragraphs or two pages for writing assignments. When kids veer from the assigned topic and add random pieces of information, it can look like they are trying to fill the space. They might get stuck on certain details and repeat them over and over in different ways. Not because they have nothing more to say, but because they are stuck! Coming up with content may not be the problem. If they can't organize content in their head and get it on the page, the paper they write will *not* represent what they know or want to tell you.

   Not knowing *how* to start can make a simple writing assignment an all-out battle, and each paragraph is another starting point that requires this skill. The area of the brain that specializes in writing and word processing is the same as for executive skills. The difficulty they have with planning, organization, and initiation will absolutely affect their ability to communicate effectively through their writing.

   Think of what goes into writing. First, they need to come up with an idea, even if the subject is provided. If the topic is motivating, this step can be easier, but there is a lot left to do before anyone can understand what they are trying to convey.

   Then they need to come up with the details that must be related enough to support the topic, yet different enough to demonstrate a thorough knowledge of the subject. These different details need to be organized so that they are set apart from each other.

Finally, they must remember all this while the brain instructs the hand in how to form or type the many letters that will express this brilliant concept.

Who knew writing was such a complicated process! By the way, this process pretty much covers most of the skills that reside in the frontal lobe. If this area of the brain isn't completely developed, it will throw off the entire process... even if the idea, interest, and cognition are there!

- **Difficulty ignoring irrelevant information**. Often it is hard to move past random information that might make its way into writing essays. Reading and trying to pick out the relevant details can be very tricky. If the topic is about the impact of war on society and the article goes into more information related to the bombers, the plane might be enough of a distraction to affect the detail that was remembered. When the reading comprehension test is given, their response might make it appear like this child didn't bother to read, they just looked at the pictures.

- **Homework**. If the assignment isn't written down or the materials never make it home, there is no way to complete homework. When homework is repeatedly not done or handed in on time, points can be taken off because it is late or incomplete. Now this child who may be exceptionally good at science is getting a D because of the many points they have missed from not handing in their work. This grade now reflects their executive functioning, not content mastery.

- **Working in a group.** Interactive learning is a big part of education today. If your child struggles to read the room, focus on a goal, start a task, or take turns, these group assignments will be painful. Many bright kids have trouble showing their full potential when they must now navigate the social aspect of a group assignment.

- **Behavior.** Behavior issues can occur for many reasons. Some kids are never told "no" or they are left on their own because parents aren't available. Either problem will affect how this child feels about adults and this will show in their behavior. Some kids just don't feel good or they may be experiencing sensory problems, anxiety, hunger, or they didn't get enough sleep. Many behavior-related issues stem from lagging developmental skills that make it hard to control behavior. When kids don't have the right skills for the given situation, behavioral regulation will be very tough. This occurs whether we are talking about a six-year-old or a sixteen-year-old. Brain development is responsible for skill development, and if the skills aren't there, this child will not find fun or success. Executive skills are always a huge part of the puzzle.

This is not an extensive list of all the various ways skill weaknesses affect school performance and behavior, but it will give you an understanding and provide possible insight into your child's struggle at school. The level to which school and home are affected depends on your child's wiring and the gap between the demands and skills; the bigger the gap, the harder it is. Some kids can hold it together at school only to show their struggle at home while others can't hold it together at all and this will affect *everything*.

Now what? What can we do to support our child in school? Is there a way parents can help in this process or is it just the teacher? There are so many different considerations when looking at your child's behavior when they are out in that big world and away from home. The next section will discuss some strategies that support the development and management of executive functioning in school. You can share these ideas and concepts with your child's teachers *and* implement a lot of the ideas at home. Some is relevant to the classroom environment but a lot of it can happen at home with homework and to support the expectations for learning in school. You may not be sitting in class with your child, but your support in this process and collaboration with their teacher will make all the difference in their academic success.

STRATEGIES FOR EXECUTIVE FUNCTIONING IN SCHOOL

It makes sense that executive functioning skills mature as the brain develops and this development takes time. The skills will also be affected by individual wiring because exposure to different things improves skills. Wiring often determines what a child can handle so this will often set the stage for what they will and won't tolerate. Sensory processing issues or signal imbalances affect some kids, but we know that executive functioning and the thinking brain is under-developed in *all* children. Brain development, no matter how much therapy, exposure, or practice we provide, will still take time. Just like when your toddler was learning to walk, you could push, pull, lead, and cheer them on all day, but they walked when they were ready.

Like soccer or any other complex set of skills, we *can* improve function with exposure, teaching, and practice. The more we allow our child to practice or execute, the better. There will be some people who develop certain skills faster, but the strategies for executive functioning really could be applied to all kids because all kids have developing brains.

How can we improve these skills? Sometimes, we simply wait. Other times, we need to loan them *our* thinking brain because they just aren't ready for the skill or activity they are attempting. The three areas we can tackle to help with brain development and resultant skills include:

1. Modify their environment
2. Change the activity
3. Improve their skills through teaching, coaching and guiding

This section will cover ideas for improving executive functioning at school and also at home for homework. Many issues arise at home because when they walk through the door after a long day, they are tired. Their brain is tired. But now they need to do homework. The school environment is full of structure, consistency and people that are more likely to keep your child's attention than what they can focus on at home. When all of their friends are working on math, they probably will too.

When the teacher asks them to do something, there's a better chance this will happen than if a parent asks. Behavioral regulation and participation at school is important and most kids can hold it together at school only to completely fall apart at home with homework.

1. **MODIFY THEIR ENVIRONMENT.** If we can adjust their environment, much like we do with sensory issues, we will often see that a child can find success and confidence. We know that sensory issues require awareness and environmental modification so we must be cognizant of too much vs. too little stimulation when coming up with ideas. Helping with skill development is similar. They may need more or less input to be able to respond successfully. Organizational strategies help to simplify and establish order in an external space because it may not be happening in their internal space also known as their thinking brain.

REMOVE and simplify. Here we want to pay attention to extra stimulation and the actual space they are trying to work in. Like issues with too many signals, if we can make their space safe and simple, the dragon won't shoot signals that are distracting and annoying.

- Reduce noise distraction. Use white noise or music that they find soothing or helpful for centering emotions and attention.
- Make a work station in a place with less *visual* stimuli like in a corner with very little clutter on the wall and a clean work space. Be aware of the lighting! They sell glare shades that can go over fluorescent lights, or you can adjust the lighting with lamps vs. overhead lighting.
- Allow for frequent breaks and remove the expectation that they can sit and work until the whole activity is complete. Chunking work helps kids realize they can complete what you've asked. Use a timer, focus on only a few problems, and always talk about what it looks like when they are done.
- Consider your expectations. Sometimes adjusting expectations and focusing on the process can improve the journey. Try to

find the just-right-challenge to prevent shut down, but give them something realistic to reach.

- Take out any extra things that don't help with comfort or focused attention. Remember, many teens like to lie on beds or couches, and this helps them focus unlike the neck ache I get after five minutes in this position. Rigid, traditional chairs and desks might not work, so find what your child likes and then see if it works.

- A separate space away from the bedroom is also a good idea. The dining room or guest room doesn't have the many fun items that live in their bedroom. Creating a space that they design might be just what they need to increase the work cycle at home.

ADD things. Create more stimulation, provide more signals, and provide tools when skills aren't adequate. We have to continue to address signals *and* skills because we need the signals before the use of skills is even initiated.

- Provide cues for task initiation, such as a little bell or noise that is out of the ordinary, to signal that it is time to start. There are also focusing apps to help them self-monitor and determine how long their focused attention can last.

- Write on sticky notes or make dry erase lists on the mirror to provide visual reinforcements or reminders. Schedules, checklists, or anything that allows items to be crossed off are great ways to *feel* productive.

- Set alarms or reminders that utilize technology. Smartphone technology has made life a lot easier for people who don't get internal signals. Have kids show you how to set up alarms. They will have buy-in because it will be their knowledge that set it up, and they will be excited to demonstrate a proficient skill especially if you aren't good at all the technology stuff!

- All of the things related to the sensory system can increase signals by adjusting the environment. Oil diffusers add smell, movement and heavy work add proprioception, and fidget tools and anything oral provide touch input.

- Create spaces that allow kids to see what is coming, track their time so they can pace work which also helps them start work, and plan what is next. When they can see the steps of the day or that task, their planning skills improve. When they time themselves to complete four problems, they just increased focused attention.
- Have headphones or space for kids to dictate their ideas with technology vs. writing them. Kids can get really good at editing this material, and now all the thoughts they had are on the page for you to see.
- Put class materials in one place of the room, so if they forgot an item, they can independently get what they need instead of always asking for help. Eventually we might notice that they don't even need the supply corner. But at least for now they have the materials they need to learn and participate in class.
- Create a different work space with all the items needed for homework completion.
- Put sticky notes with the steps of an assignment right on their desk so they can cross things off that they have completed.

ORGANIZE. Bins or folders make it easy for them to externally organize their materials, prompt for reminders, and make chaos more manageable.

- Place needed tools such as pencils, paper, etc. on a wall-mounted unit, so the items are always available but not in the way.
- Hang up a schedule that shows the chunks of time and make sure the breaks and fun stuff is scheduled too! Even when kids know their schedule, this can be a point of reference to look at for improved motivation and focus. The motivator is right there, *after* math. At home, they see the chunk of free time in the evening as long as they get their work done. When they lose focus and homework takes an extra hour, that free time disappears. This can help to reinforce the importance of focus but remember, this will not mean success. When we dangle a reward and they still can't perform we *must* look at ways to change how they are doing things. They might need more frequent breaks, more movement, music, etc.

- See-through bins and colored folders that are easily accessible but not in the way will allow kids to visually see the math, in the red folder, that needs to be completed.

- Have a box or file cabinet with accessible places to put items they are working on. They may need your help with this because categorizing and organizing skills aren't always easy. Have a space for TO DO and DONE. If they have questions on something, have them stop and put it in the QUESTION pile until they can ask for help. If they can continue to work even though they are stuck on something, they will have more to cross off the list and feel *accomplished* which feels very different than *stuck*.

- Use a whiteboard for easy erasing whether working on problems or managing a to-do list. Try a whiteboard as the writing surface. They now have a doodle space right at their fingertips and they won't keep ripping the paper as they write on a scratched dining room table.

2. **CHANGE THE ACTIVITY OR TASK.** Adjusting how a task is done or what is expected can be a huge relief for kids who never feel successful. We want to make sure we don't do too much, but there will be times when we simply need to adjust things. We can push harder once they've found success.

- Make tasks shorter and build in frequent breaks.
- Allow for extra time to complete something and try using a timer.
- Break apart big projects or assignments and make them into manageable chunks.
- Cover up most of the page and only show the line(s) they should finish. This can help them start and continue until the last problem. You can also highlight the chunk they need to do.
- Provide motivators or rewards for work completed.
- Avoid busy work! There will be times when busy work makes an hour of homework take an entire evening. Busy work is important for some kids who need repetition for mastery, but if your child doesn't need this level of repetition, consider having

them demonstrate a few problems and let them be done. Most teachers are open to this conversation from parents.

- Do the writing for them or allow them to dictate using technology. Sometimes just getting them started by doing some of the writing when you know they have had enough can give them momentum. Dictation is a tool that is easily accessible with today's technology in our school system. Dictating to you or into a device might actually improve the learning process. They will get better at editing and can cover more material than if they were writing all of it themselves, all of the time.

- A note for teachers: It is interesting to see how much more content students absorb when the notes are provided and they can highlight or add to them. Some kids need to just listen during lectures. Listening, absorbing, and writing can often be too much. When kids can listen without the motor demand of writing, the stress level goes down and the brain works! If they don't have to stress over getting all the details on the page, they might digest more. These notes you provide are actually legible compared to the chicken scratch they find on their page, so this is even another perk!

3. IMPROVE THEIR SKILLS THROUGH TEACHING, HELPING OR COACHING.

Help build skill development through exposure, teaching, and practice similar to how we might coach athletics. Remember that executive skills are no different than any other kind of skill. They improve with practice. Practice can be critical, but sometimes kids can trick us into believing that they understand all the steps and pieces when they really are missing more than you think. They may miss critical parts because of a lack of focus, trouble writing and listening, or any other myriad of reasons. If they miss a part of the instruction, they will struggle to independently complete a request. Again, getting on their level and talking to them about the problem solving can help you better understand the real issue at hand.

Sometimes we simply need to loan our frontal lobe to them because the skills aren't as mature as other areas. This is especially true of gifted thinkers. They are undeniably smart, but there may be other areas like writing, that prevent them from showing what they know or even starting an assignment. Some kids miss instruction because they can't write fast enough, or write and listen at the same time. When we can take out pieces and allow for less to *do* in the moment of struggle, they will still benefit from the content but won't be limited due to lagging executive skills. Let them dictate their answer so they can edit it later. At least their thoughts will now be on the page. Show them *how* to do something… model the process, model the behavior. Even though they think they know, ask questions like "what might come next" or "how do you think you might get there?" Maybe they show you? This process might require that we are asking the right questions. It definitely means we need to constantly keep our emotions in check so learning can happen. Anxiety over the essay they still haven't written isn't going to help them write it. Loan them your brain for the moment so they can just get started.

If we don't have a concept of time, it's hard to plan or execute. Today is tricky because technology has allowed us the convenience of instant everything. We don't have to watch ads, we get instant messaging, and we can look anything up at any time with an almost immediate response. Play today is different too, so these skills aren't forming through imaginative play that requires the concept of time. We need to have a concept of time for our plan to make sense. Teaching kids how time feels is yet another executive functioning skill. Luckily, this one is easy to teach with the use of an analog clock. Just marking on it with a dry erase pen to show how long they estimate something might take will help them begin to visualize what time looks like and how they are doing with estimating time.

> I remember when I was a kid, my mom would say, "Brush your teeth during the commercial". We knew what this felt like because we had to sit through many ads before our show would come back on. My kids wouldn't have the slightest idea how long to brush! Would yours?

Procrastination is a common issue for kids who have weak executive skills. We see this in kids with the concept of time and planning.

They must be able to plan before actually starting or they won't have the materials needed and will likely face many distractions every time they get up to get a pencil or another drink of water. There's a great time tracker app called "360 Thinking" from Kristen Jacobsen and Sarah Ward, the founders of Cognitive Connections. It gives a visual for different chunks of time so you can estimate how long something might take. The work cycle in their process involves the three steps of GET READY, DO, and DONE. These are shown with a clear visual on the clock and each is color coded: GET READY is yellow, DO is green and DONE is red. DONE is where the motivation comes in so we can create some false dopamine by talking about it first. It is important to plan backward before starting the execution because we need the motivation that comes with seeing what they can do when they are DONE. The next area of planning is for the GET READY.

My son always struggled with this one. He would come up with so many reasons to leave his workspace only to return 45 minutes later because he got distracted by the Legos he walked by after leaving the kitchen. If it takes longer to do work than your child anticipated, they will see that the DONE time gets shorter. When fun time isn't as long, they may be motivated to figure out why. This is a great visual for improved understanding and self-monitoring with natural consequences to distractions or poor planning.

Plan Backward to Move Forward

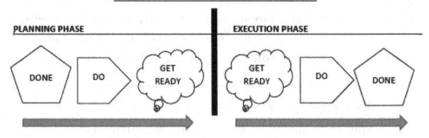

Adapted from a Concept of Cognitive Connections (Sarah Ward & Kristen Jacobson)

A big desk calendar and some sticky notes provide great visuals for teaching time and planning. This is an easy way to make a visual schedule that is flexible. First go through your child's work for the week. Break apart anything that is long so each of these chunks can be addressed separately.

Write all the steps they need to do for homework, one at a time, on the sticky notes. Things that aren't negotiable should be written right on the calendar itself, like doctor appointments, sports practice, or family events.

When you begin the conversation about their week and how to plan out their homework, you can put these sticky notes on the calendar but then move them as you plan. They will also be moved as you review the previous day's work. If they didn't finish the first paragraph they had planned to finish last night, this sticky note moves to today, then tomorrow, and so on. When there is a pileup of sticky notes on a certain day, these kids now see what procrastination looks. That video game that was too fun to stop doesn't seem so fun now that the entire paper has to be written tonight instead of just one paragraph. They may need help chunking it apart, and now you have created a visual way to show these chunks.

Suddenly they can *see* what procrastination does to a plan instead of living it and having a complete meltdown Thursday night. When a child sees five sticky notes on one day, you can talk about what that might feel like rather than living it, and you can re-plan, so that day or week looks better. The "what if" discussions during these planning sessions are important for meltdown prevention. This seems obvious to us because we have a clear picture of what procrastination feels like and how it happens… we've been through it. They haven't.

Checklists and clear schedules that show what is coming are beneficial for everyone, but kids may not know how to do this or understand why it might help. Our world gets busier every day, and teaching this skill will likely create a lifelong strategy. If the steps to skill attainment aren't easy, these kids won't try on their own. Try to be as specific as possible and repeat the instructions and/or provide written instructions to refer to later.

Remember too, that kids will have a different way of doing it than you or their sibling. If it works, the way it looks doesn't matter. We can share our ideas with them to try, but if they don't work, have the child suggest their ideas. Anytime we can help kids with organizational strategies to let them see *how* to plan or organize, they will be able to navigate their world with more success and independence. Many adults don't even realize how critical an organized and clean workspace is for attention and task initiation. Kids have even less experience and this can be a vital starting point for them. Consistency with only *one* organizational method is really important too.

> I had a paper calendar, a schedule in my phone, post-it notes everywhere, and a random notebook for TO DO items. When someone needed something I never had what I needed so I felt even more scattered. Once I got everything in *one* place, with *one* system, I was more organized and felt more efficient.
>
> Thanks Debb Oliver

A problem some kids encounter relates to getting stuck. They put words into these writing organizers, but then they have nothing else to say, so they copy those few words to their page and are left with very little content. Those few words were designed to be a reminder, but this child is stuck and has nothing else to write. If a picture is drawn quickly, even one that is unrecognizable to someone else, the brain and imagination can usually come up with more content. Now the child doesn't copy just these exact words onto their paper. Instead, they are looking at a picture that represents the idea they want to talk about.

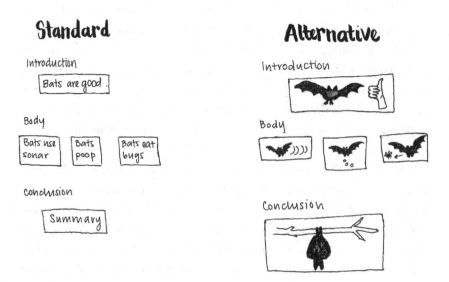

Looking up pictures on the internet is another quick way to help them start the process of writing. Have a sticky note on the desk by the computer. The note can have a word on it but then they search for pictures related to that word and write down the things they think of when they see different pictures. Now the content from these sticky notes is more complete and can be used in a more successful writing experience. So many ideas form with images that might not happen with words, and it can be a fun way to begin the work cycle.

Pictures work for parenting and expectations too. When we explain something to a child, we are expecting that they heard us, have a visual image like ours, and can now complete what we are requesting. But many times they haven't heard us or all of the instructions. Most of the time when we make a request, the picture in their head is often different than ours. How do we ensure that everyone is on the same page? How do I know if my expectation is appropriate for this task? Why is my child *never* doing what I ask or how I asked him to do it? Take a picture of the end result: a clean room, a finished sandwich, the steps of brushing teeth. All of this ensures that everyone has the same idea in mind and it also provides a reference for kids who might miss critical steps to a task.

If you have a kid who loves Legos, you know how those things can get absolutely everywhere! My son's room was a complete disaster on a regular basis, and when I asked him to clean it, he would go in and return 5 minutes later. He was done. Upon further inspection, we discovered that everything seemed to magically land in his closet or under his bed. When I told him to try again, he looked confused. We did it together and soon he realized that "clean your room" includes under the bed *and* the closet…

BUMMER!

When it was all clean, I took a picture. The following week when the room was hit by the same Lego hurricane, I showed him the picture of his clean room. This time instead of saying, "Clean your room," I said, "Make your room look like this." Suffice it to say, this was no five-minute feat. I quickly realized that my expectations and the end result picture in my head of "clean your room" was *very* different than the one in his head.

Thank you, Sarah Ward for this tip!

EXECUTIVE FUNCTIONING AND COACHING

Coaching is one of the greatest ways to help develop executive skills while still supporting that brain during its development. It can be done at school or at home. Similar to a coach for athletics, the adult is the guide but the child must do the execution. You can help with the plan and goals, but the actual *doing* must come from the child.

Coaching involves a quick daily check-in to go over classes, homework, goals, and progress. Sometimes it can happen quickly at school if you have the support and a teacher, counselor, or other adults who can chat with them in the last five minutes of their day. Parents can coach their kids, but the emotional piece needs to be observed continuously. Children shut down when parents are stressing about what hasn't been done, and this can negatively affect the relationship. Sometimes an outside person is required.

Ultimately, a coach helps the child see or create a plan. Strategies and occasional setbacks are discussed so the child can learn from the *process*. If things get negatively emotional, people tend to go into fight or flight and then into complete shut-down. Nothing gets done, everyone is miserable, and the child is to blame and has failed you, yet again. Many nights may end like this. But don't give up. Try to stay positive and emotionless.

Initially, you want to prompt the child with:

1. What did you do in English?
2. Do you have any homework?
3. What did you do in Math?
4. Do you have any homework? etc.

Run through all the classes every day. They need to put themselves back in that setting so they can remember what was going on and if there was homework, because planners usually aren't used by most kids. In the beginning you will do the writing on a calendar and put it in a place they won't miss seeing it. I like a large calendar, planner, sticky note or even dry erase marker on the bathroom mirror. Let your child be the guide for what they think will work. It may take a couple of tries, but if they have control they will have more buy-in. Remember that kids will have a different way of doing it than you or a sibling does. If it works, the way it looks doesn't matter. I have tried so many cool planner options with my kids only to find all my effort and time crammed behind the bed with nothing written on the beautifully designed pages.

Make the beginning of this process easy on them so they will talk to you and understand the process. Eventually, we want them to manage their calendar or schedule on their own, but until the habits are changed, this aspect of coaching is critical!

Some tricks I've figured out through working with these kids are:

- Put up a large desk calendar on the wall of their room. They have to walk by it every time they leave. Don't forget to attach a pencil, because if they have to go find one, they won't bother. Put big things on the calendar so they can see what other things will be coming their way, like visits to Grama's house or a volleyball game.
- Electronic planners and reminder lists work well. They can put in chimes, reminders, and different ways of sharing information with the family calendar to ensure that everyone knows what is going on.
- Taking a picture of homework on the board is another trick so they don't have to write down the homework in the last ten seconds of class when everyone is packing up.
- Use *one*, bright-colored folder that goes to every single class. Label one side TO DO and the other TURN IN. Make sure this folder goes everywhere and is pulled out during each class and during the coaching sessions. Having one consistent folder also allows them to get into the habit of using it. Some kids have pencil cases attached to these binders because they often lose their supplies. Many kids also have computers that are required to go everywhere. Help them find a way to carry this folder with the computer so they always have a place to put those extra papers that need filing. The TO DO side of the folder can also have things that need to be dealt with later at home later.

OTHER ISSUES

WHEN STRATEGIES ARE NOT ENOUGH

This next section discusses issues that likely won't be remedied with just strategies. Sometimes there is more going on, and knowing how to assess the situation for bigger problems is critical. The internet puts so much information at our fingertips, so knowing what to search can help you decide if you need more help. Educate yourself, try out some strategies, but know when to get help. Some kids, no matter how much they love dragon talk, will still be stuck even when you are using every trick and communication tool out there. This book is not meant to take the place of therapy. It is intended to provide knowledge and a different way to look at your child, but this is not always enough. The following will summarize some problems that likely require outside intervention, whether by an OT, speech therapist, physical therapist, or other type of specialist. This will hopefully give you some jargon to share with your pediatrician if you are concerned there is more going on.

Auditory Processing- This can look like a signal issue or a sleepy dragon but may be related to how the brain is processing sounds or language. Auditory processing disorders can affect how concepts and thoughts are retained, so repeating instructions aren't as helpful as saying something a different way. Their hearing may be fine, but understanding and processing language concepts can be challenging or take a long time. Sometimes it is difficult to distinguish between motor planning and auditory processing, so if you see difficulty with follow-through on instructions, you might want to consult an OT or Speech Pathologist.

Visual Perception- These skills will affect everything we do visually, and can affect a child's ability to read fluidly, comprehend what they are reading, and quickly process information that is read. There are many different skill areas, but if your child is always frustrated reading or finding something hidden in a lot of visual detail, you may be dealing with visual perception instead of a signal issue.

Dyslexia- There are many undiagnosed cases of dyslexia that can be subtle and affect reading and maybe even writing, spelling and speaking. When kids struggle to read despite having the intellect to be much better readers, dyslexia may be the issue. Dyslexia is a learning disorder that involves confusion of letter order, difficulty identifying speech sounds, and understanding how those sounds are used in speech. They might not understand what they read, may struggle with sight words, and can't sound out words easily. Dyslexia affects areas of the brain that process language. There are optometrists who specialize in visual function for learning, and some schools even do a screening for dyslexia in kindergarten and first grade.

Visual Scanning- When the brain has to tell the eyes *how* to scan across the page, it is harder to remember what was read, so comprehension will be poor. This is seen a lot with kids who weren't on their tummies as babies or didn't like to crawl. Fusion of vision is essentially the skill of both eyes working together, and this doesn't generally develop until age eight. This can explain difficulty with reading before that age. But remember those developmental timelines. A child with ADHD might be developmentally delayed by three years, so now we are looking at skills that might come in at age eleven! Children might skip words or lines or completely lose their place unless they are pointing to each word which makes reading very slow. If visual scanning isn't smooth, the eyes can get lost on the page, and reading will be slow with poor comprehension. If you suspect your child has trouble with visual scanning, there are many amazing pediatric ophthalmologists who specialize in diagnosing and treating this problem. Frustration and poor behavior related to reading or reading time might be more visual scanning than regulation.

Irlen Syndrome- This is a problem with the brain's processing of visual information. This can include light sensitivity, problems with reading, learning, headaches, or migraines. The brain can be overstimulated when reading black print on white paper. Symptoms include blurry vision, words that move on the page, or seeing a halo around words. Visit Irlen.com for more information.

Dysgraphia- This is a learning disability that makes writing very challenging. It can affect spelling, or word spacing and sizing, but what most people report is a problem with legibility. Writing can be slow, poorly organized, missing punctuation and capitalization. Dysgraphia is a learning disability that affects the physical act of writing and most kids with dysgraphia avoid writing at all cost. Sometimes kids can show neat and legible writing but it takes a long time. Others might struggle with listening *and* writing so notes in class are illegible. If your child has constant messy work that always needs to be redone, it might be related to dysgraphia.

Processing speed- Processing speed is relevant to finding success for many reasons. It affects a child's ability to meet our expectations, and significantly influences their response to our demands. Much of this is related to wiring.

- Faster processing might mean there is no need for a lot of repetition. "Thinking on your toes" can make life faster, but there are some downfalls too. Due dates, critical steps, and thoughts can be missed when the brain is processing too quickly. My son can process really quickly so he doesn't need to spend as much time on math. His wiring makes him efficient in this manner, but he tends to miss details with this efficiency, so he will miss parts of the instruction and his work is often incomplete.
- Slower processing might mean more time is needed for a response and this can make people think kids aren't listening. An advantage of slower processing is that there is time to see more detail and weigh options. My daughter needs a little more time, so math might take longer, but she is thorough and rarely misses the detailed steps.

Remind your child, no matter how fast or slow they might process, there are strengths to each. If we can see the good, we can figure out how to make our wiring work for us.

Processing speed can also be affected by exposure and repetition. As a child grows, their nervous system is evolving, and experiences are molding how this child will receive, interpret, and respond to this experience. Kids who are sitting and looking at a screen are experiencing very different input than the one in the back yard making a mud pie. The nervous system becomes accustomed to the experiences we are exposed to and this will affect how the body communicates with the brain. When more senses are used, such as when making mud pies, a solid pathway is created. Sensory information can get up to the brain for analysis with more speed and efficiency because of repeated exposure and lots of experience. We need these signals for our thinking brain to do its job.

- When we play with mud a lot and use our touch or tactile system, we create a solid pathway more like a freeway. Information can pass quickly without any roadblocks straight to signal central.
- When we are not experiencing mud on a regular basis, those tactile pathways to the brain don't get used enough so the roadway is not anything like the freeway. Every time this kiddo touches mud, or something equally mushy, the body sends messages that arrive late or damaged so the fire dragon gets concerned. This could be dangerous! Why else would these signals be this confusing?

It stands to reason that the more we repeat an experience, the better the pathway between the body and brain. Our wiring and threshold for input determine how much balance we can find in order to learn from the experiences around us, and subsequently process sensory input.

Gifted Brains- Many times we assume that when kids are bright, they must be competent. This is often quite the opposite because work production and focused attention are common issues that impact success. If they figured out how to do the problem twenty minutes ago, they likely aren't still focused on math. But gifted brains are wired very differently, and many times there are skills that don't develop when we would expect them to. Their math skills can be amazing, but reading the emotions of their friend might be underdeveloped. Just because kids are smart doesn't mean their executive skills are further developed than their peers' skills. Gifted brains have asynchronous development, which means that things develop at *very* different times.

Expectations can be one of the biggest hurdles for these kids because with a high IQ comes a higher expectation for potential. It is often assumed that they should also be motivated, focused or able to get work done quickly. When these kids struggle, it is usually because they have yet to fully develop certain executive skills. They are smart, but they may not be able to start a project that is easy and well within their ability level. They may not follow through or finish the work cycle, which means that they have a C in class when everyone knows they understand the content. They may not want to go to social events or they rarely talk about a special friend because they really can't read the room, so they may not make friends easily or they seem more immature. Remember, just because they are smart doesn't mean they are good at everything. The *why* is still just as important to figure out if you are trying to understand why your child hates school or has no friends.

Sensory Processing Disorder (SPD)-

SPD is very much an invisible neurological disorder, and understanding the different areas is critical for understanding the behaviors you will see. The

> "The hallmark of children with Sensory Processing Disorder is that their sensory difficulties are chronic and disrupt their everyday life. Children with SPD get stuck."
>
> - Lucy Miller

difference here is the severity. Kids with SPD are stuck to the point of not being able to manage the dragon, no matter how hard they try. You can practice over and over, test strategies, and dissect the very nature of signals and how they affect behavior, but these kids stay stuck. This may mean that a child may not eat, or will eat only brown food. Major meltdowns may follow any situation that requires wearing shoes. Family outings or fun play with friends might have you walking on eggshells because these times never end well. Superglue might be needed because the dishes, vases and anything fragile are never safe when your child is in the room.

Sensory processing issues are very different than threshold needs that affect regulation. No one has a perfect sensory system that works for them all the time, but when you are dealing with SPD, all those parenting techniques you try, no matter how consistent or brilliant, don't help unstick this child.

- If someone can't control their legs and they are confined to a wheelchair, we would never expect them to run across the field because we know that their body and nervous system won't sustain this activity. SPD is the same, but it isn't as easy to *see*.
- If a child experiences extreme pain with light touch, we won't see this as easily as we might see the wheelchair. We might even have the response of "toughen up" or "get over it." We might view this child as weak or sensitive when really their nervous system is sending so many signals it feels like a razor just cut their arm. They may act like they don't care or don't want to be around peers, but they may be protecting their system from input that creates a negative sensation.
- If a child doesn't sense how their body moves through space, they might break everything in their path. They can appear clumsy or even become the class clown because their behavior was once funny and this child desperately needs a friend. Little did anyone know they just didn't know where their body was so they missed the chair when they went to sit; the embarrassment made them pretend like they did it on purpose.

SPD is very complicated, and some of the strategies used will be similar to what has been presented in these pages, so there is no harm in trying ideas right now. But if things don't get better, it might be time to reach out for more help. The earlier treatment can happen, the easier behavior is to manage. The entire family unit and village of people in this child's life need to understand that this child likely has no control over their behavior. More than ever, it is critical to look at this child through a different lens.

They need our patience and kindness. Remember that everyone has a purpose and a path... some just need a little more time and maybe a lot more help.

We've established that behavior drives every relationship we have, and every interaction with a child will be affected by your assumption of the *why*. When sensory processing issues are present, a child's behavior may appear purposeful when really it is their nervous system trying to achieve balance. You may be looking at a child who is just trying to survive in a world that is not designed for how they are wired. Suddenly words like lazy, unmotivated, temperamental, daydreaming, disrespectful, or not working to their potential are used to describe this child. We can all have bad days, but if there are more bad days than good, there is likely an underlying issue that hasn't been identified, and it may be responsible for the behavior and lack of emotional control we are seeing.

Lucy Miller wrote <u>Sensational Kids,</u> a book which beautifully summarizes how a sensory processing disorder differs from merely a personality trait or a sensory preference. There are many books, online resources, and therapists who can help. Awareness is the first step, and knowing where your child struggles will give you words to describe *how* they struggle. There are three main areas of sensory processing disorders, and similar to threshold issues, they will manifest in different behaviors that make life challenging. The only difference here is that the symptoms appear to be life-altering. The following will briefly summarize the various aspects of Sensory Processing Disorders (SPD) as defined by the Sensory Therapies and Research Center (STAR) founded by Lucy Miller.

SENSORY MODULATION DISORDER:

This will affect <u>*how*</u> the child responds to input or signals. They might over-respond or do nothing, and it is very similar to how the signals work in the system. The thinking brain is only as good as the information it is fed. It won't work if the signals aren't working.

Lots of signals mean a big, fast, urgent response is needed, so all the troops are called out. We see behavior that is loud, fast, forceful, and usually not appropriate for the setting they are in or for what they are trying to do.

No signal? Well, that one is pretty easy. Nothing happens. They don't answer questions, they forget to do what they are asked, or they are too forceful because there are no signals telling them that they have pushed hard enough.

There are three ways signals affect behavior.

- <u>Over-responders</u> have way too many signals and this causes the child to over-respond to *everything*.
- <u>Under-responders</u> have too few signals which causes the child to miss what is going on around them... all the time.
- <u>Sensory cravers</u> need extreme input and often don't calm down after they get it.

SENSORY DISCRIMINATION DISORDER:

This is primarily a *signal issue*. Like a bad game of telephone, there is a signal, but details aren't coming through accurately, so the thinking brain has to do the best it can with what it is given. When the signal doesn't communicate the details that affect the response, we get behavior that isn't regulated, or is different than we expect. This can occur with *all* eight senses:

- Visual. They might not catch visual detail or might misjudge the depth of something.
- Auditory. They might not hear certain parts of the instruction or sounds.
- Tactile/touch. They might not accurately feel the item and this affects motor skills.
- Gustatory/taste. They might not differentiate food from glue.
- Olfactory/smell. They might over or under-respond to certain smells.
- Proprioception are sensors in our body telling us where our body is, how much force we should use, etc. They might not know they just gave a super hard high-five.

- Vestibular relates to the sensors in our head/ears telling us where we are, if our head is tipping, or if we are moving, etc. They might not know they are falling, or how they are moving.
- Interoception relates to sensors in our body telling us how things feel. They might not know they need to use the bathroom.

Often these kids will get lost or have trouble finding their way around a building that others can easily navigate. They can appear clumsy because they don't know where their body is in space. They might stomp their feet instead of walking because this is the only way they know where their feet are. They might miss the chair as they go to sit down or trip and fall because they don't know they are falling. They may need instructions repeated frequently because the mere act of controlling their body has consumed all their mental reserves.

You might see a lot of frustration with seemingly simple tasks because the signals don't have enough information to help the thinking brain. It is really hard to adjust when you don't know something is off. When the thinking brain isn't given much information, it is slow to learn and needs lots of extra time to figure out what should have been in that initial signal.

SENSORY-BASED MOTOR DISORDER:

Dyspraxia- This is a problem of, "How do I do that?" These kids have trouble coming up with a plan and carrying out movement patterns. Coordinated motor responses require a plan, and sometimes doing simple things means a lot of planning. When these seemingly simple tasks aren't easy, kids often create behaviors that distract anyone from figuring out that they don't know how to do something. We might see this child only play a certain game, or always need the rules to stay the same because change means they need a new plan. Some kids make up their own rules that get them out of the part of the game they can't do; now the obstacle course only has three things instead of six according to these new rules. Rigid behavior and difficulty with change or multiple stepped tasks can be commonplace for this child and this *will* affect the behavior we see. This can appear like a dragon issue, but it can also stem from difficulty integrating sensory information, so they are left unable to follow through with a motor activity.

A child may know where a piece goes in a puzzle but can't figure out how to rotate it to fit.

- A child might be viewed as a poor sport when really, they can't manage the many different rules required to play.
- A child might have trouble independently completing tasks like brushing teeth or a seemingly simple activity that requires sequencing steps. They may struggle with cutting out a shape, shutting a car door, or even using a fork and knife when their younger sibling has been doing it forever.
- A child might have poor eye-hand coordination and difficulty with typical kid games. They can appear clumsy and have trouble with balance or overall coordination.

Postural Disorder- This is a problem often associated with "oops." These kids battle with control of their bodies for the demands of the activity. This isn't always recognized as a disorder, so many kids are considered clumsy or absent-minded. What they are lacking is adequate signals and some way to get rid of the traffic jam along the pathway between the brain and the body so information can come in quickly. Often the issue lies in the vestibular and proprioceptive senses, so the body isn't getting accurate information about movement or from the limbs to know where it is in space.

- They might not know where they are, so when they sit down, they miss the chair.
- Behavior might be silly because then no one knows they messed up.
- They might have poor balance, strength and posture or have trouble using both hands together.

PARENTING RESOURCES

WHEN STRATEGIES AREN'T WORKING

It is clear that sensory processing, thresholds, and wiring can severely affect our signals and how we behave, perform, and feel about our world and ourselves. Brain development is a critical component in executive functioning and this directly affects *everything*. It doesn't matter if you understand all the ins and outs of sensory processing issues or the skills related to brain development. Maybe you don't know how to explain to your child's teacher that you think there is something legitimate going on that your child can't control. What matters is that you know you are not alone.

Part of my motivation in writing this book was because it is easy to feel alone in the struggle. When I would talk to parents who were dealing with the same issues I was at home, it helped me to know that my kids aren't all that different or messed up! I could see the light at the end of the tunnel.

The most important thing to remember here is reframing. These are not bad kids. We are dealing with a very real issue that can make it hard for them to find success. What can we do?

We've established that movement and heavy work is critical. Having a clear, visual picture of what is coming in their world can also help them be more organized and direct their energy. We need to help the people in their world understand who they are. Allow enough wait time. Observe and respect your child's needs and preferences. Don't be ashamed, embarrassed or in denial of the struggle. Everyone, including your child, knows failure is *no fun*!

Regulation is critical, but chances are we have created habits and rituals that have permeated the *why* of behavior. This means *one* solution will not always work. Strategies, tools and knowledge are important but *how* we engage with our kids is the framework around all that we do. This is where parenting resources or approaches are so important. We can help our child feel better in their own skin, but if we keep falling back into our behavioral patterns of walking on eggshells or making peace, we are enabling behavioral choices that *will not work* in the real world. We now need to change gears and focus on *how* we are approaching problems.

Wiring is critical when it comes to how we feel. My daughter's wiring left her with an active dragon who was always needing her attention. My son's dragon left him with unfinished work, late assignments, lots of fun but never that feeling of true accomplishment or success. Controlling their dragons helped make every day feel better.

Whether your child has trouble controlling their body, their behavior, or if life just seems hard, good self-esteem is the outcome that most parents want their children to achieve. Parenting resources are everywhere, but let's be honest, kids can be tough, and this parenting job is even tougher. Figuring these kids out is only the first step. Then we need a plan for what to do! I haven't invented anything new. Instead, I have tried to tap into as many wonderful resources as I can for help. In the process of figuring out the why of behavior, I've come across some amazing approaches that have helped me tremendously, both with my kids and with the kids I see in my practice.

Here are a few specific approaches that I have used. Keep in mind there are many more amazing programs and professionals not listed here. As a parent, I just needed something besides time-outs because my kid was sitting in time-out an awful lot! I needed a starting point with a positive approach because I was so overwhelmed and emotionally exhausted from all the dragons in my house.

- **Love and Logic:** This is a wonderful parenting approach that provides natural consequences for behavior. When my kids were little, I used this the most. It is easy to implement, and I was exceedingly tired in those days. I needed easy. I ordered the videos and books and could quickly implement ideas. The title is exactly what it suggests. You love your child enough to set limits, but you use logic to allow your child to experience natural and logical consequences for their behavior. Empathy is a big piece of this approach, and it helps to nourish the child-parent relationship.

Real life is full of natural consequences, so teaching them early can be very beneficial.

> When your child comes barreling into the kitchen and knocks over the glass of juice, likely for the 200th time, do you think sitting in the corner will calm them down? Probably not! Love and Logic uses an "energy drain" which helps the child see that this behavior has drained the parent's energy. If a child's poor behavior means the parent can't do their job, it is now up to the child to help their parent.

- **The Nurtured Heart Approach:** This is another positive parenting program that focuses on giving your energy to the behavior you want to see. When I looked at how a simple argument began between my two kids, I realized that my good intentions were completely missing the mark. If one kid hits another, I might address the kid who did the hitting and ask them to stop or try to redirect their behavior. If the situation escalated, so did I and so did my energy. Where did all this energy go? Yes, to the offender. The poor kid who got hit and is being quiet or has left the room got none of my energy. They have responded in a way that I wanted, but still they got nothing. Reframing and focusing on the kid who made the better choice is hard, but eventually the offender saw that it was more fun to get my energy than a consequence. The fun that comes with good behavior can mold behavior. This approach is very effective for intense children and those with oppositional defiance and attentional deficits. The goal is to simply to reframe the behavior as inner greatness that has yet to be realized, not to change the child.

- **Lives in the Balance and Dr. Greene's approach:** Dr. Greene says, "Kids do well if they can." His approach looks at executive functioning and more explanations of the possible *why* of behavior. He has written many books that give examples of how to implement his approach through the ALSUP (Assessment of Lagging Skills and Unsolved Problems), and he takes into consideration the child's perspective for the problem-solving. He has written books like <u>The Explosive Child</u>, <u>Lost at School</u>, and <u>Lost and Found</u> and writes about specific ways to help kids who struggle.

I work with and live with kids who have trouble focusing. You know, those "squirrel moments" that make it impossible to teach them anything? When I say, "Pay attention" or "stop talking" I have subtly put them down and done nothing positive toward helping them use their superpower of enthusiasm and observation for good.

Start with a positive. "I see your eagle eyes are hard at work again." I've pointed out to everyone that this child has a keen ability to observe things… pretty good for self-esteem. Spin the dragon talk and point out that they need to use those eagle eyes and ears to help the dragon see more and listen more too. Eventually, they may only need the positive remark as an indicator that they have lost focus and are having a "squirrel moment" again.

SELF-ESTEEM AND CHILDREN: HOW TO FOCUS ON THE POSITIVE

When your child focuses on the negatives or what they *can't* do, it prevents them from embracing their self-worth. Sometimes we need to help them see how amazing they are. Isn't this why we use dragons? Everyone has traits that are amazing, and sometimes these traits make it hard for us to find success in *all* situations. Rather than disciplining all the time, telling them what they have done wrong, or telling them to stop, try to focus on how a trait is amazing, and work together to help them find success.

It can be tough to focus on the positive when you are exhausted from the behaviors you currently live with. Dragons are exhausting! Seeing your child for their strengths takes practice because the negative is so incredibly memorable… for everyone. Try to start with two positives for every negative that might need work. It helps you see good in an otherwise rough situation and doesn't result in fight or flight quite as quickly. It can be hard to change your approach. It can be hard to ignore the negative and try to *find* the positive. Even if you don't say it aloud, just having a mindset of positive can usually affect the way you talk to your child.

CATCHING THE POSITIVE: We all remember moments of success when we made someone happy or proud, and kids really need this. Shifting our perspective to the positive allows us to provide tools instead of criticism. Dopamine drives the brain's reward system, and it controls motivation and the feeling of well-being that allows for learning to happen. Constant monitoring of negative can result in fight or flight, which makes learning impossible. Dopamine can increase through setting *realistic* goals and achieving them… kids need help with this process. When we get the behavior we want and attention is given to that behavior, it is remembered and we will see this behavior again. If they *could* behave, they *would*. We are dealing with brain chemicals, and we need to find the best way to address behavior.

When a child has reached the just-right-challenge and we point this out to *other* people, the impact is huge! When I know the child is in ear shot and I brag about them to someone else, this helps instill a sense of pride because what they did was good enough to share, and now others know how awesome they are.

FOCUS ON THE GOOD STUFF: Ask your child to think of a positive and something they *can* do. Just shifting the way we think can make a huge difference. I have had clients start a Book of Positives. This can be done at home, but if they are struggling at school, this could easily be something the teacher can help them with too. Make sure the things in this book focus on specifics like, "I did the dishes and took out the trash" because there is *specific* input about a *specific* task that might have been challenging. When they begin the self-doubt that often bubbles up, you can look back at this journal as proof that their dragon *can* be trained, and maybe the messages your child is getting right now are wrong. Perhaps the issue is temporary because there is proof that poor behavior doesn't *always* happen.

Often noticing just one simple positive thing can make a smile show up. Modeling this is powerful too. Make comments in front of them that show them how to embrace positive. This doesn't have to be mind-blowing, just positive and realistic.

- Celebrate even the little successes
- Share *your* successes
- Practice scenarios and listen to different ways other people would deal with them

FIND A WORD FOR THE YEAR: I have always been terrible at New Year Resolutions. I forget, or they are too hard. Think of ONE word. One word is easier to remember, and it can be used in so many ways. Post this word on an easy to see place to remember what to focus on. As the year goes on, I bet this word will apply to more situations! (Thank you, Dori Draper!)

BREATHE:
Breathe when I'm upset at my child's behavior and before I respond
Breathe when I am doing too many things at work and need to slow down

Breathe when I am walking and need to release stress

Breathe when I want to focus or find mindfulness

ACCEPT:

Accept compliments

Accept criticism and know it isn't bad, just an opportunity for direction

Accept that I can change what isn't working

Accept that my child is not like I am, but they are perfect just as
they are

BE CAREFUL WITH THE NEGATIVE: Helping children develop
self-belief and self-esteem involves self-talk, but it's also critical to watch
what you and others say. Avoid using negative labels such as clumsy, hyper,
or stubborn. Remember that behavior is often a result of wiring or coping
mechanisms, so spinning it in a positive direction can help kids begin the
process of self-monitoring. We want to guide them toward strategies and
problem solving. Don't let people label your child and if they do, help them
spin it in a more positive manner. Hyper can be enthusiastic or energetic.
Aggressive can be assertive. Unpredictable can be flexible.

When we ask a child to stop doing something and nothing happens,
it may be because this behavior is their attempt at regulation. If talking
a lot or tapping their pencil is related to their wiring and we insist they
stop, we may be going against *who* this child is, and *how* they are wired. In
addition, the more we focus on expectations that are too high or strategies
we think they should use, the less we can help. When success is too hard
to achieve, kids tend to give up because what the adult wants to see is
essentially unattainable. Goals must be realistic for *this* child, and we must
help them find the just-right-challenge.

If consequences don't change behavior, we need to change our
approach. If their room is still a disaster after nagging and taking away
television, consider that maybe they don't know where to start. If they are
talking or humming during quiet work time, maybe we need to replace
this behavior with oral input to focus. When we don't consider the *why*
of behavior, we end up with diminished self-esteem and focusing on yet
another way they have failed us.

- If disruptive behavior can be ignored or redirected to a strategy, they may be able to adjust behavior.
- If attention can be given to the child who is demonstrating appropriate behavior, they are caught being good and it will make a clear impression of what desired behavior looks like.
- Recovery after a disruption or poor choice is important to focus on after a mistake. We can briefly acknowledge the bad, but focus more on the recovery and plan for success.

> *IF WE FOCUS ON THE POSITIVE, WE WILL GET MORE POSITIVE BEHAVIOR*

TABLE OF AWARENESS: One way I attempt to focus on the positive is through a Table of Awareness. We want to find a goal to that supports and guides behavior, but first we must be aware of two crucial things.

1. *Wiring,* or who this child is. This won't change. If wiring can be thought of in a positive manner, that is how we should think of it. Hyper could be active or excited. Lazy could be observant. Stubborn could be intelligence or leadership ability. Sometimes there is no way to spin things positively, so just try to be honest but not judgmental. A short attention span is what it is. Impulsivity is excitement, but it also means that it is hard to wait. Are they a quick learner, or do they have trouble waiting? There is a big difference so call it what it is so you can find a solution that is realistic, but use kind eyes.

2. *Strengths,* or what is working for them. These are usually easy to discuss because they are already positives. Sometimes the strengths you see at home are harder to see at school, or vice versa. But these are areas we need to identify because they will help us override the negative during times of difficulty.

Once these two areas have been identified, think of a goal. The goal area is usually related to where the child is struggling. The goal should be specific, and if the child is able to participate in this part of the process, all the better. The child is the one who feels the struggle, so considering their input helps with buy-in and control. We want to address what is motivating for the child. Goals and awareness can be for school or home behaviors, and this is why the child is so important in the process. Parents don't often know how things are going at school until behavior is extreme enough to receive that phone call or teacher conference. The following is an example of how this table can look for your child.

TABLE OF AWARENESS FOR STRATEGIES

BEHAVIORS/WIRING	STRENGTHS	GOALS
Impulsive	Eager to help, enjoys being independent	Listen to all steps of instruction or use a strategy to remember steps and complete on their own
Excitement and zest for life (almost puppy-like; fun and positive)	Positive, creative, kind and empathetic, excited with new activities	Find strategies that help decrease interrupting when someone talks
Limited attention span	Engaged and is often listening even when it doesn't look that way, often asks for help	Use tools to increase follow-through with homework or chores
Difficulty reading peers and adjusting to their non-verbal cues. Often engaged in peer arguments and are frequently getting in trouble	Enjoys peers and likes to make others laugh. Doesn't seek extra attention, but does enjoy it	Learn to wait, observe, plan and then execute. May need help with any of these steps

CONSEQUENCES ARE STILL VITAL

Kids will be kids. This means that while you might try really hard to find an explanation for their behavior, sometimes there just isn't one. Kids also need boundaries, structure and discipline to mold behavior, and natural consequences are a perfect way to do this. It is vital however to first understand and consider all the factors that affect behavior because if you are missing something significant, your reaction to your child might be the one thing that completely shuts them down. It is really hard to mold behavior when your child doesn't care anymore.

Try to think through the various things you now know about the *why* of behavior. If you find something that makes sense, you can tackle that part of the puzzle.

- First, rule out possible signal issues. Are there too many? Not enough? What about sensory need that should be addressed like sleep, hunger, and pain. Their environment will affect their behavior based on their wiring and threshold. Is there too much going on? Not enough? Is there something about an activity that is setting off signals or putting them into fight, flight, or freeze?
- Next, think of the skills and the demands of the situation. How big is that gap between skills and expectations? Are they able to do what you are asking? Have you given them enough time to respond? Do they understand the directions? Maybe a list in addition to the instructions would ensure they don't miss any steps.
- Finally, revisit what you know about *who* your child is. How they are wired, how they communicate, what their strengths are, and their self-confidence will *all* affect how they are able to respond. Maybe they have a motor issue like not knowing how hard they are pushing on something so this is why that high-five was so hard. If there is a learning issue, they might not remember what they read so the list of twenty questions is impossible for them to answer. Are they always in fight or flight at the thought of new things?

Once all of this has been considered, it is time to discuss boundaries and structure. Knowing the rules and having consequences when they are broken is how we create boundaries and structure. Even if your child has signal or skill issues, natural consequences help them learn the process and significance of their behavior. The real world can't adapt to their needs all of the time so they need to *feel* the natural consequences when they make mistakes. It is still important to help them examine if their system prevented them from making good choices and they still need guidance for strategies and tools but they also need consequences.

All kids will manipulate, and *all* kids will show frustration and misbehave… even *we* do! This journey of parenthood is a dance and one of the biggest ways to prevent your child from finding success in life is through learned helplessness. If you do too much to solve their problems or make life too easy and buffer them from feeling the natural consequences of their actions, they will continue to blame you when things go wrong. They need to make the connection that their behavior resulted in what they are feeling right now. You can still support them and empathize with their struggle, but as hard as it is for *you* to experience, *they* must feel the struggle.

Parenting is a dance and this I have learned through the process of trying to understand how my son's brain works. He has ADHD and there are times he absolutely *cannot* focus. I have come into his bedroom many times to see one computer screen with YouTube, one with a car race, and headphones playing music while he is doing his calculus homework. He tells me that this "unacceptable" way of doing homework is the only way he can keep his brain focused. And it works for him.

The dance now shifts.

I have to acknowledge that this technique works for him, but he has to get his work done. If he doesn't, maybe he tries my way. Maybe he can't go see friends because his work isn't done.

This is how the dance goes. Back and forth.

Always with respect and logical consequences.

As mentioned in the beginning of the book, this isn't linear; there are many steps and detours. Sometimes there won't be an explanation for what you are seeing. Natural consequences are real life. "Because I said so" is not a natural consequence. Missing dessert because they forgot to brush their teeth again is a logical consequence that fits the behavior. Sympathizing and listening to them vent about missing recess because they didn't get a test done lets them know you care about them, but you also support and respect their teacher and the rules at school. The struggle can also help their skills to further develop because they still need to be pushed. The just-right-challenge means they can find success, but are still challenged. This challenge can be tough. Structure, boundaries and follow through can be difficult. The dance shifts again to include challenge without shutdown. You shouldn't care or hurt more than they do. Their struggle will result in learning as long as it is logically related to the behavior. You can totally master the steps of this involved dance!

OTHER CONSIDERATIONS WHEN DEALING WITH BEHAVIOR

- Teach kids that fair doesn't always mean the same or equal. We all get what we *need*, and sometimes that looks different. Teaching the value of differences allows for empathy, tolerance, and ultimately happiness.

- If you are implementing consequences over and over and nothing is changing, you are probably not dealing with the true problem affecting their behavior. Remember, if we don't hear the problem from the child's perspective, we may not be addressing the root of their behavior. Helping a child understand their perspective and advocate for their own needs is a tremendous life skill that will help them everywhere. Guiding this process can be a lengthy and exhausting feat, but well worth it in the end.

- While technology can be an excellent tool, it should be just that. Encouraging your child to find something without an electrical plug develops aspects of their foundation upon which other skills develop. Exploration, social engagement, moving our bodies, and learning to hang out and just *be* is critical. *Doing* is essential and some of us get very good at always doing. But it's all about moderation. We need the tools and foundation to be able to both *be* and *do*.

- Examine the situation. Misbehavior usually means something is off. Is your child feeling out of control? Is there something setting them off that is just too much? Are our expectations more than what they have in their toolbox? Have we really listened to them… taken the time, without a screen or interruptions, to *really* listen? Sometimes that is all they need… *our time and attention.*

- Behavior evolves over time, and it is dependent upon what came before. Parenting is one of the hardest jobs out there, and it is possible that we don't have the right tools in our toolbox. Consider getting more strategies for your arsenal or trying to adjust your perspective. It is okay to admit you were wrong or made a poor choice. Children need to see that adults make mistakes too, but they also need to see that how we respond is what really matters. Be honest about your struggles and how you got through them.

- Time is our most precious gift. Try to take a minimum of two hours before jumping in with an assumption or a lecture. If you are having trouble with your emotions, this will let your brain see the big picture. Time is a great perspective changer. Remember too, that everyone has a different timer. I know that my husband needs 24 hours before he can even have a serious, emotional conversation. If I push him too fast and don't respect this, the conversation will *not* end well. I can verbally process right away, but he needs time to process and think.

- We are all in this together, but *everyone* needs help sometimes. Talk to your child, talk to your spouse, talk to your friends, talk to your dog. Let people into your world and ask for help.

SUMMARY

I have met many incredible parents, teachers, caregivers, and kids on my journey as a therapist and a mom. If you are lucky enough to have other people in your world who love your child, you already know that it truly takes a village to raise a child. It takes the patience and love of everyone in that child's life. Sometimes all it takes is a different way to look at a situation to make you realize that this too shall pass. Maybe it doesn't matter if they are in all AP (advanced placement) classes if it is destroying the journey.

Step back and refocus. What matters is the connections we have with each other. These connections come from acceptance and learning, and most importantly, understanding. As a parent, I want one thing for my children. Happiness. Happiness is a life-long goal and dependent on the journey and all that is discovered along the way. If we can tuck our kids in after a long, hard day, and they are still smiling and confiding in us, we have done them the biggest service of all.

Sometimes when we are wrapped up in our child's difficulties or tears it is hard to remember what really matters. In twenty years, no one will remember if your child had trouble sitting still or making perfect cursive letters, but they will remember the smiles, the laughter, and the lessons that each of us must learn on the course of this incredible journey.

Even a wink or smile will increase the effect an adult can have on a child because they might feel for a moment that they have been seen for *who* they are and not what they do. It will let the child know they are valued, no matter what kind of wiring they have. We have an opportunity, especially when kids are young, to help them embrace who they are, be proud of it, and then maybe problem-solve how to make their wiring work in the real world. It can be hard, and life may be hard. So much can happen when just one special person sees the good this child can bring to the world.

If they COULD, they WOULD. Success is way more fun than failure (Thank you, Dr. Greene)

> Things will get better, whether through strategies or understanding. You will likely need both! We need to understand our own wiring to help our child navigate their issues because otherwise emotions and behavior can get out of control and nothing gets better.
>
> We only have a short time with our children, so remembering to not sweat the small stuff and enjoy *who* they are is something you will never regret!

Remember that most of what keeps us awake tonight will pass. What will impact your child the most is the relationship you have with them and the understanding that you are there as a guide. We don't want to create learned helplessness, but we know children develop self-esteem and confidence when they feel unconditionally supported. Take the time to consider some different explanations for behavior. Trying to figure out *why* your child is struggling will be a huge step toward "Happy".

If you remember nothing else, I highly recommend the eight second hug that I mentioned at the very beginning of this book. Being available and in the moment with a child allows for an opportunity to get to know them better and for them to know you better.

I know that I am only a guide for my children, but in many ways they have been a tremendous guide for me. It is humbling to do, but allowing yourself to really listen to children can provide some of the most valuable lessons for self-growth. I don't know if my children were chosen for me, but I can definitely say that I have gotten as much from them as I hope they have gained from me.

I hope some of the ideas in this book provided a little insight to help you.

You hold the key to much of the power that will allow you to find beauty and love in a way that perhaps you didn't yesterday. Thank you for your commitment to our children… they are our biggest asset for the future!

For more information, consultation or for training purposes, please contact me at:
Kristin Robison, MOT, OTR/L
Secrettohappy.com
secrettohappy@gmail.com

QUICK LIST OF STRATEGIES

Wait time: Make sure you have given enough time for processing AND responding. This can range from 3-10 seconds depending on your child and how much they are facing.

Make a picture or word schedule that shows the major events of the day or task: This will provide a quick, easy clue that doesn't require the brain to work, which will help to simplify what we are asking their brain to do.

Break up activities that are difficult or multi-stepped: When the page is visually busy you can cover some of it up so they only have to focus on the part they should work on.

Play and move bodies before work: Many people think movement and what they might consider "play" is for *after* work, but most people need to move their bodies before working.

Sports, exercise, jobs, and chores: Movement and heavy work into muscles feed the nervous system with effects that can last 2-6 hours. Incorporate this input into their daily routine.

Foster calmness: Speak with a low volume and pace.

Avoid Fight or Flight: Our protective system kicks in when we have gotten too much input for what we can integrate.

Structure: If your child knows the general sequence of the events in their day, they can better anticipate and prepare for it.

Deep pressure, heavy work, and movement: These are critical for regulation.

Respect anxiety, preferences, and fear: These are real and usually based within the nervous system… it may not be under the child's control.

Get creative: The goal is to feed the nervous system by utilizing the sensory system and providing for movement, force or pressure, heavy work, or by stimulating the senses.

Control: When behavior problems occur, children are usually feeling out of control. When you give them an opportunity to control something, behavior usually gets better. It can be as simple as making a deal with your child during homework. Maybe they choose the next break activity when they work through a certain number of problems. Make sure the choices you give them are all acceptable to you so they will be successful no matter what they choose.

WE can help *all kids* find success!

ACKNOWLEDGMENTS

It is really scary to write a book about your own children, about your experiences both personal and professional, and about kids who are struggling. There will always be people who disagree with your recommendations, and there are very unique circumstances that make some strategies work one day and not the next. Along the road of sharing my story and experiences, I was lucky enough to have support, laughter, and insight that made this book what I wanted it to be. It is all about the people... the village. My village has so many incredible people that weren't listed in these pages but who made this process and my sanity possible. It is these individuals I wish to thank.

My mom, Betty Christianson Martinsen, read every single word at least 15 times over to make sure it was correct. My husband, let me constantly bounce things off him, even though I just said the same thing five minutes ago. My kids, Jens and Annika, are so incredible and gave me permission to share personal details to help others. Thank you to Deb Oliver for her vision, expertise and business management and for always getting me into the most incredible opportunities. To Miya Mackenzie for her amazing marketing ability and wordsmithing for every aspect of this project. I so appreciate the "Think Tank" of Miya, Peggy Borgeman, Molly Dahl and Deb. Trisha Sagare designed my cover quite possibly 600 times and never complained; she somehow knew what I wanted before I even did. To my sister Julie Broxson who is one of the most amazing marriage and family therapists, thank you for sharing your insight and ideas. My sister, Janel Ulrich, helped me wordsmith because titles are really, really hard to come up with. Speaking of titles, thank you to Miya Mackenzie (and Trina), Carrie Ayarbe Fields, my mom, Heidi Ayarbe, Sydney Fields and Deb Oliver and so many more who helped me with words until I finally landed on something I wanted, that told the essence of this book.

It is so hard to mention everyone along this path; it has been a project of seven long years, and truthfully more of a hobby until I realized it might actually be fun to publish. The entire Carson City School District, its administrators, teachers, paraprofessionals and students gave me support, enthusiasm and were always my cheerleader. My sister-in-law, Sudie Jones, Chelise Crookshanks, Carrie, and numerous parents of clients have been my "beta readers" and I have so appreciated their feedback. To my amazing village of friends, I thank you from the bottom of my heart for your friendship, encouragement and insight. Every hike and glass of wine that eventually turned into a "therapy session" affected my perception and ultimately the words that ended up on the page. A very special thank you to Carly Syndergaard who shared her beautiful gift of words and journey as a parent in a way that perfectly complimented the content of this book.

I am thankful for all the positive energy and people in my world who are kind, giving and just trying to make a better life for their families and those around them. We must always remember that we are in this together and the road is much more fun with people beside you.

RESOURCES

Amen, Daniel G. *Healing ADD: The Breakthrough Program That Allows You to See and Heal the 6 Types of Attention Deficit Disorder.* Putnam's, 2001.

Biel, Lindsey, and Nancy K. Peske. *Raising a Sensory Smart Child: The Definitive Handbook for Helping Your Child with Sensory Processing Issues.* Penguin Books, 2018.

Bundy, Anita C., et al. *Sensory Integration: Theory and Practice.* F.A. Davis, 2002.

Dennison, Paul E. *Switching on: The Whole Brain Answer to Dyslexia.* Edu-Kinesthetics, 1981.

Dunn, Winnie. "Supporting Children to Participate Successfully in Everyday Life by Using Sensory Processing Knowledge." *Infants & Young Children*, vol. 20, no. 2, 2007, pp. 84–101., doi:10.1097/01. iyc.0000264477.05076.5d.

Eide, Brock, and Fernette Eide. *The Mislabeled Child: How Understanding Your Child's Unique Learning Style Can Open the Door to Success.* Hyperion, 2007.

Fay, Jim, et al. *More Ideas about Parenting with Less Stress: Journal Collection Years 2000 to 2005.* Love and Logic Institute, 2005.

Glasser, Howard, and Melissa Block. *The Transforming the Intense Child Workbook: An Experiential Guide for Parents, Educators and Therapists for Learning and Implementing the Nurtured Child Approach.* Nurtured Heart Publications, 2016.

Glasser, Howard, and Jennifer Easley. *Transforming the Difficult Child: The Nurtured Heart Approach*. Center for the Difficult Child Publications, 1998.

Greene, Ross W. "ALSUP: Assessment of Lagging Skills and Unsolved Problems." *Lives in the Balance*, 0AD, www.livesinthebalance.org.

Greene, Ross W. *Lost and Found: Helping Behaviorally Challenging Students*. John Wiley & Sons, 2016.

Greene, Ross W. *Lost at School: Why Our Kids with Behavioral Challenges Are Falling through the Cracks and How We Can Help Them*. Scribner, 2014.

Heller, Sharon. *Too Loud, Too Bright, Too Fast, Too Tight: What to Do If You Are Sensory Defensive in an Overstimulating World*. Harper, 2003.

Henry, Diana A., et al. *Sensory Integration Tools for Teens: Strategies to Promote Sensory Processing*. Henry Occupational Therapy Services, 2001.

Horowitz, Lynn, and Röst Cecile C. M. *Helping Hyperactive Kids - a Sensory Integration Approach: Techniques and Tips for Parents and Professionals*. Hunter House, 2007.

Huebner, Dawn, and Bonnie Matthews. *What to Do When You Worry Too Much: A Child's Guide to Overcoming Anxiety*. Awareness Publishing Group, 2015.

Irlen, Helen. *Irlen*, 1998, irlen.com.

Kartchner, Collin. "Helping Teens Rise Above Social Media Negativity." *#SaveTheKids*, 0AD, savethekids.us.

Kranowitz, Carol Stock., and Joye Newman. *Growing an in-Sync Child: Simple, Fun Activities to Help Every Child Develop, Learn, and Grow.* Penguin Group, 2010.

Kurcinka, Mary Sheedy. *Kids, Parents, and Power Struggles: Winning for a Lifetime.* HarperCollins, 2001.

Kuypers, Leah M. *The Zones of Regulation: A Curriculum Designed to Foster Self-Regulation and Emotional Control.* Social Thinking, 2011.

Miller, Lucy J., et al. *Sensational Kids: Hope and Help for Children with Sensory Processing Disorder (SPD).* Penguin Group, 2014.

Miller, Lucy. *Sensory Processing Disorder - STAR Institute*, 0AD, www.spdstar.org.

Milne, A. A. *Winnie the Pooh.* Happy Time Books, 1986. Randolph, Shirley L., et al. *Kids Learn from the inside out: How to Enhance the Human Matrix.* Legendary Pub. Co., 1998.

Small, Roxanne. *Building Babies Better: Developing a Solid Foundation for Your Child.* Trafford Publishing, 2012.

Team, Understood. "Dysgraphia: What You Need to Know." Edited by Charles MacArthur, *Home*, 0AD, www.understood.org.

Ward, Sarah, and Kristen Jacobsen. *Cognitive Connections*, 0AD, www.efpractice.com.

Printed in the United States
By Bookmasters